HEALTH REPORTS:
DISEASES AND DISORDERS

DEPRESSION

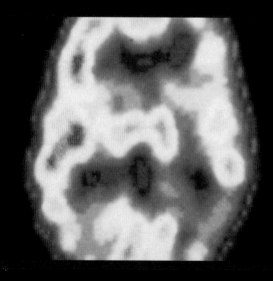

WENDY MORAGNE

 TWENTY-FIRST CENTURY BOOKS
MINNEAPOLIS

To my cherished sisters, Deverly Tadau and Lori Knopf

Cover image: These scans show a healthy brain *(left)* and a depressed brain *(right)*. The healthy brain lights up with greater activity than the depressed brain.

Twenty-First Century Books
A division of Lerner Publishing Group, Inc.
241 First Avenue North
Minneapolis, MN 55401 U.S.A.

Website address: www.lernerbooks.com

Library of Congress Cataloging-in-Publication Data

Moragne, Wendy.
    Depression / by Wendy Moragne.
        p.   cm. — (USA TODAY health reports. Diseases and disorders)
    Includes bibliographical references and index.
    ISBN 978–0–7613–5882–4 (lib. bdg. : alk. paper)
    1. Depression, Mental—Popular works. I. Title.
  RC537.M669 2011
  616.85'27—dc22   2010034122

Manufactured in the United States of America
1 – DP – 12/31/10

CONTENTS

USA TODAY
HEALTH REPORTS:
DISEASES AND DISORDERS

WHO'S WHO?

In this book, you will meet seven teenagers who faced depression and received help to overcome the symptoms of this debilitating disorder. Their stories candidly describe the powerful effect depression had on their lives and reveal the marked improvements that resulted after treatment was begun. The message these young people convey is that depression is a treatable disorder and that help is readily available.

KEVIN, 17

Kevin had never had a girlfriend before Tracey, an outgoing, fun-loving classmate. He felt more relaxed and confident when he was with her. Even Kevin's parents were happy that she was a part of his life. But after a year of dating, Tracey suddenly broke off the relationship. Devastated and confused, Kevin began to feel nothing but pain, and his daily activities began to be affected. After Kevin came home drunk one night, his parents made an appointment with a psychologist, who determined that Kevin was depressed. He began treatment with psychotherapy.

LINDSAY, 13

Lindsay's grandparents meant everything to her. Although there were several other grandchildren in the family, Lindsay had the closest relationship with her grandparents. They even lived in the same town. But when Lindsay's grandfather retired from his job, he and his wife decided to move south to a warm climate. From the day her grandparents left town, Lindsay had great difficulty accepting that they were so far away. She was used to seeing them every day. Although

Lindsay phoned her grandparents regularly, things were not the same. Lindsay's parents told her that they, too, found the adjustment difficult but that they all had to get over it. Within a couple of weeks, Lindsay's parents, sister, and brother seemed to be okay with the change. But Lindsay could not get on with her life. Lindsay began to overeat and gain weight. She would awaken during the night and not be able to fall back to sleep. In the morning, she would begin the day in a sour mood and would get into arguments with her mother over trivial things. These arguments usually escalated to screaming matches and ended with Lindsay being given a punishment by the time she left for school. She would often respond with comments such as "Go ahead and punish me. I don't care. You hate me anyway."

At school Lindsay began to have trouble concentrating during class. She also suffered from headaches and asked to see the nurse

Depression can make it difficult for people to concentrate on their daily activities, such as school and work.

so often that the nurse phoned her parents and recommended that Lindsay be checked by the family's pediatrician. After asking Lindsay questions about her health and what was going on in her life, the doctor suggested that she meet with a psychologist. The psychologist found that Lindsay was depressed and recommended treatment through psychotherapy sessions.

SHARON, 16

Sharon and her older sister were opposites. Sharon was shy and serious, while Kathy was outgoing and carefree. Sharon was overweight and had what she thought were unflattering features, while Kathy was petite and pretty. Although Sharon and Kathy got along, Sharon felt inferior to her sister because she had many friends. Sharon, on the other hand, was constantly teased by her classmates for being large. At home Sharon's parents seemed pleased with Kathy and critical of Sharon, and they urged Sharon to try to lose weight. Sharon was now in tenth grade, and many of the girls in her class were being asked out on dates. Kathy, an eleventh grader, seemed to have a date every weekend. As the school year progressed, Sharon began to feel worse and worse about herself. She felt embarrassed over the way she looked, and she felt intimidated by the popularity of her older sister. Strong feelings of self-hate and worthlessness began to envelop her. Sharon decided to diet. She ate small portions at lunch at school and with her family at dinner. Her parents expressed their approval that she was making an effort to lose weight. But Sharon could not stop thinking about food. Eating had always made her feel better. It helped relax and soothe her during stressful times. After school, when no one was home, she began to binge on large amounts of food. After these binges, feelings of guilt and disgust set in.

Sharon learned to rid her body of the extra food by making herself vomit. She would go into the bathroom and do it quietly. Eating large amounts of food and then making herself vomit soon became a habit that she could not control, but she kept it a secret.

Sharon began to withdraw emotionally more and more from her family and from their activities. When she did interact with them, she was irritable and melancholy and complained of being tired. She also complained of being bored with the things that were going on in her everyday life. She stopped going to a drawing and painting class that she had always enjoyed at the art center. Her parents considered this just a phase that Sharon was going through. But when Sharon suddenly stopped doing her homework and quit the school chorus, Sharon's parents began to realize that Sharon had a problem. They sought help from a psychologist, who diagnosed Sharon with depression and discovered that she also suffered from bulimia, an eating disorder. She referred Sharon to a psychiatrist, who prescribed medication and set up regular psychotherapy sessions for her.

JORDYNN, 14

Although Jordynn's parents were divorced, Jordynn always dreamed that they would get back together someday. When her mother decided to marry another man, Jordynn anticipated the wedding with anxiety and afterward became increasingly withdrawn and sad. Her mother grew concerned after Jordynn lost weight, had problems completing her school assignments, and complained of stomachaches. She made an appointment with the pediatrician. After finding nothing wrong with Jordynn, the doctor recommended that she be evaluated by a psychiatrist, who determined that she was depressed. The psychiatrist also diagnosed Jordynn with obsessive-compulsive disorder. She began treatment with medication and psychotherapy.

DOUG, 15

Doug had always been a good student and had many friends. But when his parents divorced, Doug's behavior changed. His father transferred to a job out of state. Because of the distance involved, he was able to visit with the children only one weekend a month. The visits were difficult. When Doug and his brother went to their father's place, the trip took three hours each way. And when Doug's father visited with them in their town, they had to meet at a public place or in their father's hotel room.

Doug blamed his mother for the breakup of the marriage. He took out his anger and frustration by arguing with her and being verbally abusive. He also picked fights with his brother, and their arguments often escalated into shouting and punching matches. Doug's grades declined, and he began to cut class. He received detentions for this, which only worsened the problem. He began to hang out with a group of older teenagers and eventually got involved in drinking and smoking marijuana. He would come home at all hours of the night and sometimes not until the following morning. He refused to tell his mother where he had been. And when his mother attempted to ground him, he would just laugh and then leave the house. After months of hopelessly waiting for things to improve, Doug's mother made an appointment with a psychologist. But Doug refused to go. Exasperated, his mother asked for help from Doug's lacrosse coach. He was finally able to persuade Doug to see the psychologist.

The psychologist determined that Doug suffered from depression and began treating him with psychotherapy. Eventually, the psychologist felt that Doug needed medication, and she referred him to a psychiatrist. The first medication did not seem to help, so the psychiatrist switched Doug to a different medication. Within a few weeks, Doug's depression began to lift and he was more in control of his behavior. The psychiatrist met with Doug on a regular basis and asked his family to become involved in the therapy, as well.

ANTHONY, 18

Through high school, Anthony had few close friends and no dates. College was about to begin, and he was going to live away from home. Although he was looking forward to studying computer science, Anthony felt anxious about college, and he worried about living away from home. He had never spent even one night away from home.

With the help of his mother, a widow, and his uncle, Anthony made the four-hour trip to college, got settled into his dorm room, and met his roommate. The semester got off to a good start, although there was much more homework than Anthony had anticipated. He immediately immersed himself in his studies. But soon he felt stressed by trying to keep up with the mounting assignments. After a few weeks, Anthony suddenly felt on top of the world. He felt more energetic than he had ever felt in his life, and he began to keep late hours. He had his bicycle on campus, and he began to take long, late-night rides along some of the winding back roads. He had never felt stronger and more physically fit. Even after getting little sleep, he was able to continue to attend his classes. In class he began to question the accuracy of the information his professors presented. Time and again, he raised his hand to question what was being taught. He felt he knew the material better than his professors, and he felt he was smarter than his classmates.

Anthony's fellow students found Anthony obnoxious, and they avoided being in his company. His roommate began to spend less time in the dorm room, and when he was there, he wore headphones to block Anthony out. Anthony took the standoffish behavior of his classmates and roommate as confirmation that he was superior to them, and his ego swelled. But in the final weeks of the semester, everything suddenly changed. Anthony became quiet and withdrawn. His energy and enthusiasm vanished. He spent a great deal of time sleeping. He missed many classes, and when he did attend class, he was not able to absorb the material. There were times when he even fell asleep. And by the end of the semester, studying for his final exams was impossible.

When Anthony's mother arrived on campus to take Anthony home for the winter break, she was stunned to find him in bed with nothing packed to go home. She felt certain that he had mononucleosis, a contagious viral infection common among teenagers. But a visit to the doctor showed no viral infection, and the doctor recommended that Anthony see a psychiatrist. After evaluating Anthony, speaking with his mother, and phoning his roommate, the psychiatrist determined that Anthony suffered from bipolar disorder. People with this disorder experience alternating periods of extreme happiness and depression. Anthony's psychiatrist prescribed medication and recommended psychotherapy.

MOLLY, 17

Molly's mother died in a car accident. She left behind Molly, Molly's two younger sisters, her younger brother, and her father. Molly's father had a very hard time accepting his wife's death. He put his time in at work, but all the joy seemed to be gone from his life. He withdrew from everyone, including Molly and her siblings. The household chores and cooking still had to be done, and Molly took it upon herself to try to keep things going. She pined for her mother, but tried to stay strong for her father, sisters, and brother. She never talked about the grief she felt.

Molly, an honor student, continued to work hard on her schoolwork and tried to fit the household chores in between. She had enjoyed spending time with her friends before her mother's death, but she had to give up her social life because of her many family obligations. The pressure mounted as Molly struggled to keep the family afloat. She found that she missed her mother more each day. She missed talking with her, running errands with her and, above all, hugging her. As time passed, Molly saw ending her life as the only way to end the pain and suffering she was going through. She confided in a friend at school that she was feeling so down that she was considering suicide. Finally, after school one day, she swallowed a large bottle of pills. When her sister came home from school, she found Molly unconscious and called 9–1–1. Help reached her before it was too late.

Most teens do chores. But teens who are forced into unusual levels of adult responsibility can find it stressful. This stress can contribute to depression.

Molly spent time in a hospital, where she did not have to face the pressures of her home life. In the hospital, she was kept safe from suicide until treatment with medication and psychotherapy began to help her. Back at home, she continues with medication and regular visits to the psychiatrist. Molly's father has also been diagnosed with depression, and he, too, is being treated with medication and psychotherapy.

CHAPTER ONE

WHAT IS DEPRESSION?

Kevin was a model student. He put great emphasis on his studies because his parents had always pushed him and his older sister to do well in school. They expected excellent grades. Kevin had a best friend named Joe with whom he had been friends since first grade. But it was difficult for Kevin to establish other friendships because of his quiet nature.

In tenth grade, Kevin had English class with Tracey, a girl who was new to the school. Tracey always seemed to be especially nice to him, and her friendly, upbeat personality put him at ease. By spring he had finally gotten up the courage to ask her to a movie. She accepted and they had a good time. Kevin asked Tracey out a few more times over the summer, and they enjoyed each other's company. As his junior year approached, Kevin anticipated continuing to see Tracey, and a bonus was that he was going to get his driver's license.

Kevin's junior year got off to a great start. His relationship with Tracey seemed secure, and Kevin felt happy and content. When he got his driver's license in November, his parents let him borrow their car whenever he wanted. He and Tracey saw each other every weekend.

"Tracey was good for Kevin," says Kevin's mother. "She had an outgoing personality, and she helped Kevin open up to other people. He seemed more relaxed and self-confident when he was with her."

In the spring, Kevin began track practice after school and was looking forward to a strong season. He was also excited about the upcoming junior-senior prom. He bought tickets to the prom the first day they went on sale. But when he told Tracey he had bought the tickets, she said she was not going to the prom with him. She had been asked by a senior and was going with him. Kevin asked Tracey why, and she told him that she wanted to start seeing other people. Kevin was devastated and confused.

When Kevin told his parents what had happened, they said they were sorry. "I think they meant it," says Kevin. "But when they said that relationships are superficial at my age and that I would get over it and find another girlfriend, I felt like I was facing the whole thing alone. They trivialized what happened to me and didn't take it seriously. Their attitude made me feel unimportant and foolish."

Kevin's pain took a toll. He was unable to fall asleep at night. He felt restless and irritable but tired and worn out too. His stomach was in knots, and he had difficulty eating. At school he tried to act as if nothing was bothering him, but he found that he was not able to concentrate in any of his classes. At home he found it impossible to finish his homework or study for his tests. His grades began to decline. Even his athletic abilities faded.

One afternoon at track practice, the coach commented on the change in Kevin and told him to shape up. Kevin became enraged and kicked the bleachers so hard that he broke his toe and had to quit the team. Kevin's father was angry with Kevin over the incident. He had been a track star in school and expected Kevin to follow in his footsteps. Now the season was lost.

"I felt so miserable about everything," says Kevin. "I saw myself as a real loser. Nothing was working out right. I felt like nothing mattered anymore, either. When I looked into the future, all I saw was a blank wall. My friend Joe would call me to go out and do stuff, but I didn't want to. Meanwhile, my parents were telling me that I was being immature and that I should pull myself together and get on with my life. That's when I felt that I couldn't handle things anymore, so I started taking my mom's allergy medicine. It was an over-the-counter medicine that I knew I could replace without her knowing. I never overdosed on it or anything. I just followed the directions on the bottle, but it was enough to make me feel drowsy and that's what I wanted. I wouldn't take any before school, but as soon as I got home,

I would take some. And then I would fall asleep and not be aware of how bad I felt."

Kevin's grades fell sharply and brought a warning from his parents. They threatened to take away his driving privileges if his grades did not improve. "All they were worried about was that I wouldn't get into a good college," says Kevin. "But all I was worried about was how I was going to face the next day." Kevin and his parents got into heated arguments about his schoolwork, and his father accused him of being lazy. "He told me that ever since Tracey and I had broken up, I wasn't willing to put my mind to anything," says Kevin.

"He told me I wouldn't amount to anything in life. He didn't have to tell me that, though, because that's how I already felt. I felt like a failure."

Kevin was relieved when school ended. He got a summer job at a pizza parlor in town. One night Tracey came in with a date. "I felt my heart pound and I could feel my face get red," says Kevin. "I tried to stay calm. I said hello to Tracey, but she didn't say anything. She just ignored me. She was with this really big guy I had never seen before. He just ignored me, too, and the two of them went on talking and laughing together like I wasn't even there. I felt humiliated.

"That night after work, some of the guys I worked with were going out and they invited me to go along. We went to a park not far from the pizza place and met up with some other people I didn't know. One of the guys had a trunk full of beer. I drank until I vomited. I just wanted the pain to go away. I was too messed up to drive home, so one of the other guys dropped me off. My parents were still up because they were worried about me. I hadn't called to say I would be late. When they saw how messed up I was, they went ballistic."

"I was shocked and angry," says Kevin's father. "I couldn't believe Kevin would do something like that. It was so unlike him. Later, when he told us what had happened with Tracey, we knew things were *not straightening out. We knew he needed to talk to someone about what was bothering him. We didn't know how to handle the problem ourselves."*

Kevin's parents took him to see Dr. Martin, a psychologist who was experienced in working with teenagers. Dr. Martin evaluated Kevin and determined that he suffered from depression. Kevin began meeting with her in weekly psychotherapy sessions.

"I'm still not over what happened with Tracey, but Dr. Martin is helping me to see that life can go on without her," says Kevin. "She's helping me to feel more self-confident, and she's helping my parents and me to communicate better. I feel stronger inside and I know that one day I'll begin to date again. Right now, though, I don't want to put myself in that position. I don't think I'm ready for that yet. But I have moved on in some ways. I've always been interested in medicine, and I've been thinking about becoming a doctor someday. I'm doing volunteer work for the ambulance corps and I'm learning a lot. I've also met some nice people. It keeps me busy and happy."

Depressed teens need an outlet for their feelings. For many, the best option is a trusted psychologist or psychiatrist.

USA TODAY
HEALTH REPORTS:
DISEASES AND DISORDERS

WHAT IS DEPRESSION?

Depression is not simply feeling blue or disappointed or down in the dumps. It is not even the intense feeling of grief experienced after the death of someone close nor the overwhelming sadness experienced after the loss of a pet. Depression is much more complex. It is a cluster of signs and symptoms that lasts a long time and affects a person's everyday functioning. *Clinical depression* is depression that is serious enough to require a doctor's care. It is a mood disorder caused by a combination of genetic, biological, psychological, and environmental factors. It affects both the mind and the body, impacting thoughts, feelings, behavior, and physical condition.

Typically, once a person experiences an episode of depression, he or she will likely experience additional episodes, although some people experience only one major depressive episode in a lifetime. Each recurring episode tends to be worse than the one before and tends to last longer.

The good news is that with proper treatment, approximately 80 percent of people who suffer from depression can get well. Many begin to feel better in just a few weeks.

WHAT ARE THE SYMPTOMS OF DEPRESSION?

People who are depressed may feel sad or irritable or may lose interest in activities that once gave them pleasure. Many feel overly tired or anxious, and most feel worthless and hopeless. Depression can interfere with sleeping and eating and can cause headaches and stomachaches. It can cause argumentative behavior, aggression, or the desire to be alone, which strain relationships with family and friends. And it can interfere with being able to concentrate or remember, which can cause a drop in school performance. Some depressed individuals even have thoughts of death and suicide. Although many people experience some of these symptoms from time to time, it is the intensity of the symptoms and the length of time they have been present that determine whether or not depression exists.

Symptoms of depression tend to vary from one person to another. No two people experience the disorder in exactly the same way. The combination of symptoms present in one person may not be the same combination present in another person. The severity of the symptoms and the length of time they are present also vary from person to person.

When a person suffers from depression, the symptoms he or she experiences and the pain he or she feels can lead to disruptive behavior, school problems, social problems, and alcohol and drug use. Giving up a favorite sport, cutting school, or fighting with siblings may be signs of depression. Even repeatedly declining invitations to get together with friends may signal depression.

Cutting school, changes in behavior, and fighting with friends and family can be symptoms of depression.

WHO HAS DEPRESSION?

Depression occurs in people of both genders and all ages, races, and socioeconomic class. Depression occurs around the world. It affects millions of people, some more severely than others. Depression runs in families, so people who are depressed are likely to have a parent, a brother, a sister, a grandparent, an aunt, an uncle, or a cousin who also suffers from depression. Depression can often be traced through several generations of a family.

The World Health Organization (WHO) is a United Nations agency that helps governments to improve health services around the world. According to the WHO, depression affects about 121 million people worldwide. According to a 2007 report by the U.S. Centers for Disease Control and Prevention (CDC), more than one in twenty Americans twelve years of age and older (5.4 percent) suffered from depression. Through interviews with approximately five thousand people, researchers at the CDC discovered the following:

- People forty to fifty-nine years old had higher rates of depression.
- Depression was more common in women than in men.
- Non-Hispanic black people had higher rates of depression than non-Hispanic white people.
- Eighty percent of people with depression reported that their symptoms made it difficult to perform at work or school, get things done, or get along with other people.
- Only 29 percent of people with depression reported contact with a mental health professional.

ADOLESCENTS AND DEPRESSION

The December 2005 National Survey on Drug Use and Health (NSDUH) reported that 14 percent of American adolescents suffered from depression. The NSDUH showed that less than half of them received treatment. All were more than twice as likely to have used illegal drugs than young people who were not depressed.

What may appear to be normal struggles through the teenage years may actually be depression. Experts estimate that 4 percent of teenagers are depressed. Considering that the average number of students in a classroom is approximately twenty-five, the rate of depression could be thought of as one student per classroom. And the rate of depression is on the rise. Some researchers have suggested that the increase in the rate of depression may be due to changes in our culture. These changes include differences in the makeup of the family structure (more divorce, stepfamilies, and single mothers), geographic mobility (moving from one town or state to another), families living far from their extended families (grandparents, aunts, uncles, and cousins), and more mothers working outside the home (mothers spending more hours away from home). These factors contribute to greater stress and a weaker support system in the lives of many young people, which, in turn, may lead to depression in some people.

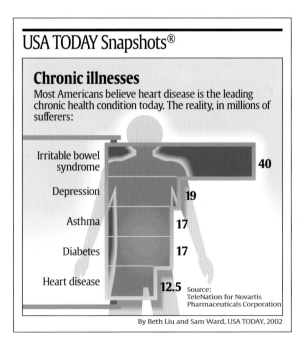

USA TODAY Snapshots®

Chronic illnesses
Most Americans believe heart disease is the leading chronic health condition today. The reality, in millions of sufferers:

Irritable bowel syndrome   40
Depression   19
Asthma   17
Diabetes   17
Heart disease   12.5

Source: TeleNation for Novartis Pharmaceuticals Corporation

By Beth Liu and Sam Ward, USA TODAY, 2002

www.usatoday.com

USA TODAY

Life

SECTION D

August 4, 2009

From the Pages of USA TODAY

Americans taking antidepressants doubles

Study: Most aren't being treated for depression

The number of Americans using antidepressants doubled in only a decade, while the number seeing psychiatrists continued to fall, a study shows.

About 10% of Americans—or 27 million people—were taking antidepressants in 2005, the last year for which data were available at the time the study was written. That's about twice the number in 1996, according to the study of nearly 50,000 children and adults in today's *Archives of General Psychiatry*. Yet the majority weren't being treated for depression. Half of those taking antidepressants used them for back pain, nerve pain, fatigue, sleep difficulties or other problems, the study says.

Among users of antidepressants, the percentage receiving psychotherapy fell from 31.5% to less than 20%, the study says. About 80% of patients were treated by doctors other than psychiatrists.

Patients today may be more likely to ask about antidepressant advertising, says study author Mark Olfson of Columbia University and the New York State Psychiatric Institute. During the study, spending on direct-to-consumer antidepressant ads increased from $32 million to $122 million.

Doctors today also are more comfortable prescribing antidepressants, partly because the newer drugs are safer and cause fewer serious side effects, says James Potash of Johns Hopkins Hospital in Baltimore [Maryland], who wasn't involved in the study.

David Spiegel of Stanford University School of Medicine says he's glad to see more people getting treatment for

HOW DOES DEPRESSION OCCUR?

The symptoms of depression result from an abnormality in the way the brain produces and maintains the levels of certain chemicals that help transmit messages from nerve cell to nerve cell. The brain is composed of billions of nerve cells, called neurons. Each of these has hundreds or thousands of interconnections with other neurons.

depression, which causes more disability than any other medical condition.

But Olfson says his study shows that doctors need more training in mental health. And he says he's concerned about the decline in patients receiving psychotherapy. Patients who receive only medication may not get the help they need, he says.

Many patients are unable to see psychiatrists, however, because of insurance barriers. Many doctors no longer accept insurance because of low reimbursement rates for therapy, Spiegel says. The study ended before the passage of a 2008 law that requires employers with more than 50 workers to provide comparable benefits for mental and medical care.

Studies suggest doctors should be cautious about prescribing antidepressants to children. In 2004, the Food and Drug Administration issued a "black box" warning that the medications could increase the risk of suicidal thoughts in children. Use of antidepressants by children fell nearly 10% the next year, according to Olfson's 2008 study of the subject. Antidepressant use had been rising so quickly in the years before the warning, however, that the rate of use in 2005 was still higher than in 1996.

—Liz Szabo

Suicidality and Antidepressant Drugs

Antidepressants increased the risk compared to placebo of suicidal thinking and behavior (suicidality) in children, adolescents, and young adults in short-term studies of major depressive disorder (MDD) and other psychiatric disorders. Anyone considering the use of Zoloft or any other antidepressant in a child, adolescent, or young adult must balance this risk with the clinical need. Short-term studies did not show an increase in the risk of suicidality with antidepressants compared to placebo in adults beyond age 24; there was a reduction in risk with antidepressants compared to placebo in adults aged 65 and older. Depression and certain other psychiatric disorders are themselves associated with increases in the risk of suicide. Patients of all ages who are started on antidepressant therapy should be monitored appropriately and observed closely for clinical worsening, suicidality, or unusual changes in behavior. Families and caregivers should be advised of the need for close observation and communication with the prescriber. Zoloft is not approved for use in pediatric patients except for patients with obsessive compulsive disorder (OCD). (See Warnings: Clinical Worsening and Suicide Risk, Precautions: Information for Patients, and Precautions: Pediatric Use)

Since 2004 this black box warning has appeared on antidepressants. It warns of the suicidal risks associated with children taking antidepressants.

Neurons in the brain communicate with one another by sending electrical signals, or messages, through axons. These are long, thin, stemlike projections found on neurons.

At the end of axons are branchlike nerve endings called dendrites that contain storage sacs that release chemicals called neurotransmitters. Neurotransmitters carry the message across the tiny fluid-filled gap, or synapse, that separates the nerve endings on the axon from the body of the next neuron. When the message crosses the synapse and reaches receptors on the next neuron, the receptors are activated, which in turn activates the neuron.

Scientists have concluded that depression involves a breakdown in this complex system, resulting in inadequate amounts of certain neurotransmitters present in the brain. The

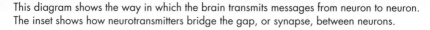
This diagram shows the way in which the brain transmits messages from neuron to neuron. The inset shows how neurotransmitters bridge the gap, or synapse, between neurons.

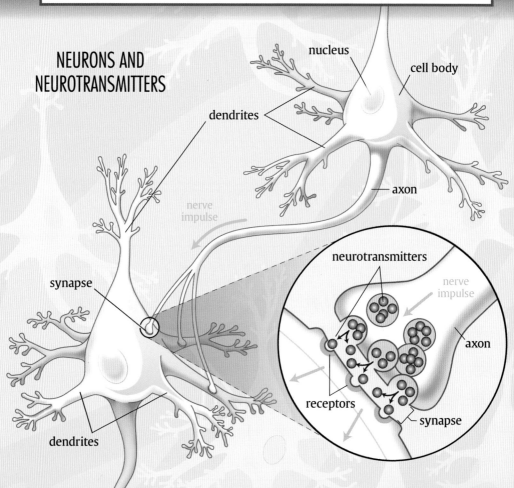

NEURONS AND NEUROTRANSMITTERS

nucleus

cell body

dendrites

axon

nerve impulse

synapse

neurotransmitters

nerve impulse

axon

receptors

synapse

dendrites

decrease in neurotransmitters is the result of neurotransmitters being destroyed after they are produced, reabsorbed after they are produced, or too few being released from the nerve endings. Scientists are still learning about how neurotransmitters function in depression. Progress is slow because the brain is complex and there are limited ways to study brain tissue without harming or destroying it.

WHAT CAUSES DEPRESSION?

Ongoing research indicates that depression is likely caused by a combination of genetic, biological, psychological, and environmental factors.

GENETIC FACTORS

Since depression tends to run in families in the same way that heart disease or diabetes does, researchers believe that some people have a genetic vulnerability to developing this disorder. Young people who have a depressed parent, grandparent, or sibling are at the greatest risk for developing depression. However, it is important to note that being at risk for developing depression does not mean that an individual is sure to develop it. Sometimes depression occurs in people who have no family history of the disorder. Heredity plays a part in a person's psychological makeup. Some people are naturally upbeat and optimistic, while others constantly look at the down side of life. Those who think pessimistically, worry excessively, and have a poor self-image may be prone to developing depression. Those who are introverted and extremely dependent on others also tend to be at greater risk.

Scientists are studying the brain and depression to find out exactly what aspect of depression is inherited. Some researchers

Depression tends to run in families. People with relatives who have depression should look out for symptoms and make sure they get the help they need.

are searching for a specific gene that, if identified, would explain why certain people develop depression while others do not. Other researchers have been studying whether certain abnormalities in the brain's chemical makeup can be passed on from generation to generation.

BIOLOGICAL FACTORS

Neurotransmitters, the brain chemicals that carry messages from one neuron to another, affect behavior, thoughts, and feelings. Norepinephrine and serotonin are the neurotransmitters that are involved in depression. When there are inadequate amounts of these chemicals in the brain, the brain cannot function properly. Norepinephrine and serotonin regulate mood. More specifically, norepinephrine regulates alertness, so when there is an inadequate amount in the brain, symptoms such as fatigue and a sad mood result. Serotonin regulates sleep, appetite, motor activity, and aggression. When there is an inadequate amount of serotonin in the brain, symptoms such as sleeplessness, irritability, and anxiety result. These are symptoms common in depression. Studies have shown that another neurotransmitter, dopamine, also affects mood. A higher level of dopamine in the brain seems to correlate with a more upbeat mood.

Research has indicated that there is a hereditary component to brain chemistry, which could explain why depression tends to run in families. If certain brain chemicals regulate mood and if problems with the way in which the brain maintains proper amounts of these chemicals can be inherited, this could explain why some people suffer from depression while others do not. Psychological and environmental factors, including negative thinking, stress, and traumatic life events, can alter the brain chemistry in certain people.

PSYCHOLOGICAL FACTORS

Teenagers tend to feel the need to fit in and to belong to a group. Having a personality that is argumentative and explosive or shy and insecure makes it difficult to form friendships and tends to limit participation in social events. The feelings of loneliness and isolation that often result can lead to poor self-esteem and depression. Young people who lack support and praise from the adults in their lives, those who are rejected by peers, and those who struggle with schoolwork often feel a sense of defeat and failure. Many feel frustrated and angry. Some become critical of themselves and see the world as a gloomy place with a dark future. Negative thinking and pessimism often lead to guilt and despair. Sometimes these young people end up feeling helpless and hopeless. They feel that things

Teens who are picked on at school or find it difficult to form friendships have higher rates of depression.

are beyond their control, and they stop trying to change things for the better. Some even lose the will to live.

ENVIRONMENTAL FACTORS

Life events can trigger depression. The death of a loved one, chronic illness of a family member, divorce, physical or sexual abuse, and poverty can bring on depression in those who are vulnerable. These hardships can even cause depression in people who do not have a family history of the disorder. Moving to a new town, pressure to get good grades, a falling-out with a friend, a breakup with a boyfriend or a girlfriend, and ridicule by classmates can also trigger depression.

Additionally, many teenagers are faced with peer pressure, sexual issues, increased responsibilities at home, and friction with parents, all of which can be stressful and may lead to depression. Occasionally, depression develops without a trigger, meaning that some people become depressed without having faced trauma or stress.

Life changes such as moving can trigger depression. The stress of making new friends and adjusting to new schools can be difficult to handle.

www.usatoday.com

Sports
SECTION C

September 2, 2010

From the Pages of USA TODAY

Giants' Andrews deals with depression;
Stigma of diagnosis difficult to overcome

Football fans understand when a player is forced to the sidelines with torn knee ligaments.

They grasp the severity of groin injuries, sports hernias and ruptured Achilles tendons.

Clinical depression?

Offensive lineman Shawn Andrews, a Pro Bowl performer for the Philadelphia Eagles in 2006 and 2007 who is making a comeback with the New York Giants, learned that many fans in the City of Brotherly Love could not empathize when he was given that diagnosis in 2008.

"I've been called everything in letters," he says. "Some of the stuff I'm even embarrassed to say. One said, 'The next time I read your name, I hope it's in an obituary.'"

Andrews recalled another fan who once asked for his autograph. The same person turned on him after he could not find it within himself to report to training camp in 2008. "You're a disgrace to the world," the man told him.

Andrews, 27, struggles to understand that response just as he once grappled with himself internally.

"We're human beings," he says. "Although some guys in this profession put up armor like 'Don't cry,' some of the guys who preach that are some of the most emotional guys behind closed doors.

"Some players came up to me and said, 'I went through the same thing. It just wasn't as public as what you went through.'"

Shawn Andrews, shown here at an Eagles training camp during his rookie season in 2005, is a professional football player who has struggled with depression.

Even as he starred at the University of Arkansas, prompting Philadelphia to take him in the first round of the 2004 draft (16th overall), Andrews could sense that all was not right with his world.

"I could see some signs even before I went pro," he says. "I didn't know what depression was. I just held a lot of things in. I didn't know who to talk to because I felt I'd get a biased opinion. So I just kept everything to myself.

"If you fill up like a balloon, it's going to bust—boom!"

According to Andrews, he took anti-depressant medication for eight months. He said his first visit to a psychiatrist helped because the doctor encouraged him to unburden himself by telling him everything that was bothering him.

"It was a relief, man. It was such a relief," Andrews says. "I'll never forget it."

Andrews looks, and insists that he feels, like a new man. He battled to keep at a reasonable playing weight for much of his college career and his time with the Eagles. Although he says his weight reached as much as 390 pounds [177 kilograms], he says he no longer drinks alcohol and is holding steady at 325 pounds [147 kg].

He is showing no ill effects after having back surgery last December that was followed by extensive rehabilitation in Los Angeles [California].

New York general manager Jerry Reese and head coach Tom Coughlin view Andrews as a worthwhile gamble.

"The quality of the football player that I remember from a couple of years ago is outstanding," Coughlin says.

The coach, concerned about the depth of his offensive line, met for 30 minutes with the veteran before the Giants signed him Aug. 20.

"He's just a pleasant young man to visit with," Coughlin says. "He does indicate to you the kind of desire that he has to get back in the game."

Andrews smiles easily and laughs often as he speaks of a support system of relatives and close friends that he lacked before. He says he is engaged to be married and points to a photo of his 2-year-old son, JaShawn, that is taped inside his locker.

"That's my pride and joy. He so smart. He's such a good athlete," he says. "He's a cool little fellow."

Coughlin understands how difficult a position Andrews is in because he was signed so late and must take a crash course on a Giants' offense that is very different from the Eagles' West Coast system.

"He's making good progress," Coughlin says. "A lot has to be learned. He's spending almost every waking minute studying.'"

Andrews admits that his lack of familiarity with the system is resulting in tentative play.

"When you are thinking on the run, it doesn't allow you to come off with everything you have," he says. "I'm a little apprehensive. 'Do I get this guy, or do I get this guy?' I don't want to get anybody hurt. I don't want to get my quarterback hurt, and I want to keep guys off my running backs."

Knowledge will come. Abundant athleticism has always been there.

"When I can go full speed, look out," Andrews says, laughing. "Look out!"

—Tom Pedulla

TYPES OF DEPRESSION

There are several types of clinical depression. All types are characterized by intense and persistent feelings of sadness and a loss of interest in things that once were pleasurable. All forms affect an individual's daily functioning. The three main types of depression are major depression; dysthymia, or chronic depression; and bipolar disorder.

MAJOR DEPRESSION

In major depression, symptoms are intense and last two or more weeks. They occur daily, sometimes lasting for most of the day, and impair functioning. For a person to be diagnosed with major depression, symptoms cannot result from illicit or prescribed drugs or a medical condition. In some cases, an individual experiences major depression only once in a lifetime, but it usually recurs throughout a person's life.

DYSTHYMIA

Dysthymia is a milder form of depression that lasts two or more years. Dysthymia occurs gradually, and people may not be able to pinpoint when they started feeling depressed. They may also have times when they are not depressed. These "normal" periods can last up to two months. Symptoms include eating or sleeping too much or too little, fatigue, poor concentration or difficulty making decisions, low self-esteem, and hopelessness. Young people with dysthymia often appear gloomy, irritable, and angry, and they tend to complain about feeling unloved and worthless. Some people who suffer from dysthymia later develop major depression or bipolar disorder.

BIPOLAR DEPRESSION

People with bipolar disorder experience mood swings from low to high and back again. The low mood is characterized by the symptoms of major depression—sadness, irritability, loss of energy, and changes in appetite. The elevated mood is characterized by extreme happiness, great energy, a decreased need for sleep, rapid talking, grandiose ideas and plans, and inappropriate and often risky behavior. The mood swings, which are extreme, can last for days, weeks, or months.

OTHER TYPES OF DEPRESSION

ATYPICAL DEPRESSION

Atypical means "not typical." The symptoms of atypical depression are opposite those typically associated with depression. Symptoms tend to be chronic and usually begin in adolescence. Rather than feeling fatigued, individuals with atypical depression feel agitated, and rather than eating and sleeping less, they eat and sleep more. Additionally, people with this form of depression tend to be extraordinarily sensitive to rejection.

SEASONAL AFFECTIVE DISORDER

Seasonal affective disorder (SAD) seems to be related to seasonal changes in sunlight. People who suffer from this disorder typically become depressed in the fall when the hours of daylight are reduced. They begin to feel better in the spring, and they experience symptoms similar to those of atypical depression. Individuals who suffer from SAD tend to feel fatigued, sleep excessively, and have an increased appetite, especially for carbohydrates and junk food. Some researchers believe that the reduced sunlight in late fall causes a change in brain chemistry, which leads to depression. The treatment that seems to be most effective is surprisingly simple—sitting in front of a brightly lit box for about thirty minutes each day during

One treatment for a type of depression called seasonal affective disorder is light therapy. Here, a special box emits light to treat the disorder.

the winter months. The light box emits high intensity light and is designed for use by people who suffer from SAD. Mood, energy level, and concentration seem to improve as a result of light therapy. In severe cases, antidepressant medication is sometimes combined with light therapy for more effective treatment.

POSTPARTUM DEPRESSION

The term *postpartum* comes from the prefix *post* (after) and the word *parturition* (the process of giving birth). Many women become depressed after delivering a child. About 15 percent of mothers display the symptoms of major depression—insomnia, loss of appetite, and inability to function—with a focus on the baby and motherhood. Postpartum depression is the result of the hormonal changes associated with giving birth and the normal stress that comes with having a child. Women who suffer from this type of depression fear that they are bad mothers who are unable to care for their babies. Without treatment, this condition can have a negative affect on a mother's relationship with her child and she may not be able to bond with the baby. Giving birth is usually a time of joy, and women who are unable to experience this joy should seek help.

PSYCHOTIC DEPRESSION

Psychosis is a mental disorder that causes a person to lose contact with reality. Psychotics are unable to distinguish between the real world and the imaginary world. Psychotic depression is severe depression accompanied by symptoms of psychosis. These symptoms include hallucinations (seeing or hearing things that aren't really there) or delusions (irrational thoughts and fears). People with psychosis may hear "voices" and are often suicidal. Research has shown that psychotic depression is sometimes related to a loss of brain tissue.

USA TODAY

CHAPTER TWO

SIGNS AND SYMPTOMS

When a mental health professional evaluates someone for depression, he or she looks for the presence of two types of symptoms: psychological (mental or emotional) and biological (physical).

Psychological symptoms include:
- Feeling sad or irritable, or feeling frustrated and angry
- Experiencing a loss of interest in most of the activities that were once enjoyable
- Having difficulty thinking, concentrating, or making decisions
- Feeling worthless or guilty
- Having repeated thoughts of death or suicide
- Experiencing hallucinations or delusions

Biological symptoms include:
- Experiencing a change in appetite and significant increase or decrease in weight
- Having difficulty falling asleep and staying asleep at night or sleeping too much
- Feeling restless or fidgety, or experiencing slowed movements
- Feeling tired and lacking energy
- Experiencing unexplained physical ailments

A diagnosis of depression means that an individual is experiencing a cluster of these symptoms and the symptoms have been present for at least two weeks and interfere with daily activities.

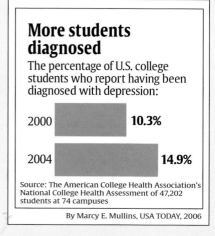

More students diagnosed

The percentage of U.S. college students who report having been diagnosed with depression:

2000 — **10.3%**

2004 — **14.9%**

Source: The American College Health Association's National College Health Assessment of 47,202 students at 74 campuses

By Marcy E. Mullins, USA TODAY, 2006

PSYCHOLOGICAL SYMPTOMS

Feeling sad, not being able to smile, and crying over things that ordinarily would not be upsetting are symptoms that some young people experience when they are depressed. But feeling aggressive, cranky, and irritable can be as much a sign of depression as feeling down in the dumps. Many depressed young people feel frustrated for no apparent reason, resulting in angry outbursts, especially at home. The anger can be directed at themselves or at others. Picking fights with family members is common. Depressed individuals also often become enveloped in feelings of loneliness and self-pity, leading to complaints such as "No one likes me" or "Life is unfair" or "Everyone is mean to me."

Depressed teens are more likely to pick fights with parents and siblings without an obvious reason.

www.usatoday.com

USA TODAY

Life

SECTION D

April 27, 2009

From the Pages of USA TODAY

More teens get screened; Doctors ask questions about depression

The next time you take your teen to a doctor for a physical, sports checkup or a minor illness, don't be surprised if the visit includes a little something extra: a screening for major depression.

Such screenings—in which teens answer a few questions about possible depression warning signs—are sure to become more common, thanks to a recent recommendation from the U.S. Preventive Services Task Force. The influential, independent panel, which is not connected with drug companies, doctors' groups or insurers, says routine depression screening should do more good than harm for kids ages 12 to 18.

Major depression affects more than 5% of teens and is linked with suicide, substance abuse and other serious problems. Yet it often goes undiagnosed and untreated, the panel says.

"If you don't ask, they won't tell," says Leslie McGuire, deputy director of the TeenScreen National Center for Mental Health Checkups at Columbia University in New York. She supports the guidelines.

But it won't be enough for doctors to just ask teens if they are depressed or to watch for outward signs, the experts say. Here's what they say a good screening should entail:

- It should be for everyone, not just clearly troubled kids. "It's something you do with a whole population to figure out who's got symptoms that might warrant a closer look," McGuire says.
- It should start with a questionnaire, on paper or a computer screen, that covers possible symptoms, such as persistent sadness, irritability and a loss of interest and pleasure in life. Several such questionnaires have been tested for accuracy.
- Teens should get a chance to fill out the form in private, in the waiting room or at home before a visit. "We tell teens that moms can't peek, there's no right or wrong answer and we aren't the mental-health police," says John Genrich, a pediatrician in Colorado Springs [Colorado] who recently started screening patients.
- It should be scored on the spot, by the doctor or office staff. Genrich says he can score the version he uses "in about 15 seconds."
- Even if the screening raises no red flags, it should be repeated occasionally. Studies have not shown how often is ideal, but "about once a year wouldn't be unreasonable,"

says Ned Calonge, task force chair and chief medical officer of the Colorado Department of Public Health and Environment.

- If the screening does raise red flags (which happens about 10% of the time, McGuire says), the provider should speak with the teen to find out more, assess any immediate danger and plan next steps—including a conversation with parents. Most troubled teens "are very relieved to have somebody share this with their parents," Genrich says.
- Teens at risk should then get a full diagnostic work-up and follow-up care—which might include tests for physical problems and referrals to mental health professionals, who might then provide psychotherapy, with or without medication.

The point of screening is not to get all depressed kids on antidepressant drugs, which have real risks, Calonge says.

And it's not to get kids into pricey psychiatrists' offices, though that will be called for in some cases, says Alan Axelson, a Pittsburgh [Pennsylvania] psychiatrist who has worked with the American Academy of Child and Adolescent Psychiatry and the American Academy of Pediatrics to better coordinate mental health care for kids. Axelson says some depressed kids will do well with counseling from a clinical social worker or psychologist, and all will benefit from follow-up with their pediatrician or family doctor.

But right now, many kids' doctors lack plans and support systems for treating and referring depressed youngsters, Calonge says. Those doctors, he says, should not start screening until they are better prepared to help.

—*Kim Painter*

Regular checkups are a good way to track mental health. Teens and their parents should use these opportunities to ask about special screening for depression and other possible mental health disorders.

Comments such as "I'm bored" or "I don't want to do that—it's dumb" or "Why bother—what's the point?" may signal depression. Many depressed young people lose interest in activities that once gave them pleasure. Some might quit a sports team while others stop taking dance or music lessons. Others decline to participate in social activities with their friends. As a result, many end up feeling lonely, which only adds to the depression. Some depressed teenagers lose interest in food and lose weight. Others seem to crave food and never feel satisfied. Junk food and foods rich in carbohydrates (cake, cookies, potato chips, and bread, for example) are especially appealing to many of these individuals. Some even hide food to be eaten later.

Paying attention and concentrating on a task are often difficult for depressed young people. Just as their body movements may seem to occur in slow motion, so may their thinking. Some may have trouble focusing on a conversation or watching an entire television program, for example. Many suffer a decline in school performance as a result of these symptoms. Others have difficulty making decisions, and they may turn to parents or other adults for help.

Depression and low self-esteem go hand in hand. Most people who suffer from depression feel that they are not as good as other people and that they are incompetent. They tend to downplay their successes but blow their failures out of proportion. "I can't do anything right" or "I'm stupid" are comments they may make. Most are overly sensitive to criticism from others. Many blame themselves and put themselves down for things that do not turn out according to plan. They view negative events, no matter how small, as proof of their shortcomings. These feelings also carry over to friendships. "Nobody wants to be friends with me" is a typical comment.

Some depressed young people become preoccupied with death. They may surround themselves with music, magazines, Internet information, and computer games that involve death or morbid themes. Some become obsessed with thoughts of killing themselves and devise a suicide plan.

Some depressed teenagers hear voices that tell them they are bad or worthless. Others have delusional thinking, involving incorrect interpretations of reality.

BIOLOGICAL SYMPTOMS

Tossing and turning after going to bed, awakening several times during the night and not being able to fall back to sleep, awakening too early in the morning, and sleeping too much are all problems associated with depression. Feeling tired upon awakening, even for those who have had enough sleep, is not uncommon.

Depression can affect the speed at which a person moves. Some individuals are restless and jittery, while others seem to be moving in slow motion. Fidgeting with clothing or hair can be a sign of depression, as can sitting idly, giving one-word answers, or speaking in monotone.

Having trouble sleeping or sleeping too much can both be symptoms of depression. Lack of sleep can also make other symptoms worse.

Many depressed people complain of feeling exhausted. Some can barely find the energy to do much more than lie on the sofa or the bed. They are often the target of angry comments such as, "You're so lazy!" or "I'm tired of you doing nothing but lying around!"

In addition to these symptoms, stomachaches or headaches that cannot be explained may also signal depression. And so may a general sense of not feeling well physically. It is not unusual for a depressed individual to make repeated visits to a doctor in an effort to find out what is causing the pain and discomfort. These ailments are often a result of feeling anxious about school performance or about being accepted by friends and classmates.

MORE THAN A CASE OF "THE BLUES"

People experience the symptoms of depression in different ways. Some may feel unhappy, weepy, and worthless and want to stay in bed all day and sleep. They may even think about death. Others may feel restless and may have trouble eating and sleeping. They may also have trouble concentrating and making decisions, and they may blame themselves for things that have not worked out right for them. When we think of depression, we tend to think of people who express sadness. As you can see from the second example, the symptoms of depression may not involve any of the emotions we associate with sadness. On the other hand, not all people who appear unhappy are suffering from depression. All of us feel sad, disappointed, and hopeless from time to time. But most of us soon turn away from the sadness and begin to focus on the people and events in our lives that bring us joy. We bounce back from the disappointment and return to the lifestyle and mood we experienced before the disappointment occurred.

For individuals who suffer from depression, however, bouncing back is difficult, if not impossible. They find it hard to get on with their lives after the event that caused them grief. Little if anything thereafter seems to feel good to them. They feel trapped in a downward spiral, and there seems to be no way out. "Everyone in my family was sad when my grandparents moved away, but they all got over it in a short time," says Lindsay. "I couldn't seem to get over it, though. I just kept feeling worse and worse as time went on. The rest of my family was going on about their business, but I was stuck in a rut."

Sometimes it is not just a single event or disappointment that causes the sadness. Sometimes it is a thread of constant hardship that weaves its way through each day and eventually takes a toll. Teasing or rejection by classmates is one example.

Being rejected by classmates would cause anyone to be sad. But for depressed teens, it can change the way they look at themselves and the entire world.

www.usatoday.com

USA TODAY

News

SECTION A

August 5, 2010

From the Pages of USA TODAY

The emotional cost

Talk among fishermen at this BP staging point each morning is a good barometer of the local mood. Early in the [Gulf of Mexico oil spill] crisis, shrimpers and oystermen recruited for cleanup work fretted that the leak would never stop. Then they worried they wouldn't get paid.

Today, fishermen here voice a fear that with the well nearly plugged, their steady BP paychecks may start disappearing.

"We don't know how long it will be before we get back to work fishing," says Donnie Campo, 46, an oysterman working for BP. "We look at what happened in Alaska and they're just starting to fish now."

The emotional rollercoaster coastal residents have ridden since the spill appears likely to continue even as the well is sealed.

Many of the fishermen of lower St. Bernard Parish [Louisiana] find themselves in a dilemma: happy that the well

Cleanup workers vacuum oil from marshes in southern Louisiana after the Gulf Coast oil spill in 2010. The long-term costs to the environment and the livelihoods and mental health of those who make their living along the coast are yet to be seen.

may finally be clogged but worried that it means BP jobs may soon vanish. A boat captain could make $2,000 a day.

"As soon as these paychecks stop and you realize you can't do anything, you're going to watch that anxiety and stress go through the roof," says George Barisich, a shrimper and oyster fisherman who leads the Louisiana United Commercial Fisherman's Association.

Oil disasters often lead to spikes in depression, anxiety, divorce and post-traumatic stress, even years after the event is resolved, says Steve Picou, an environmental sociologist at the University of South Alabama.

After the Exxon Valdez spill in Prince William Sound, Alaska, fishing communities saw a rise in suicide, divorce and anxiety for six years after the spill, and symptoms lingered for another 12 years, he says.

"In this disaster, unlike a hurricane, people cannot be rescued and there's no way to inventory the damages," he says. "You have an unfolding conveyor belt of problems."

Unlike the Alaska spill, however, the Gulf already had scores of groups created after Hurricane Katrina [in 2005] to help people recover from that disaster, Picou says. Many are shifting to helping residents deal with the spill.

Catholic Charities has opened five mental health centers across the Gulf and treated more than 6,000 people since the spill.

It sends counselors to docks and marinas to counsel fishermen. Larry Carbo, a Catholic Charities crisis counselor, says many he's spoken to have been drinking more or abusing their spouses. Others have confessed thoughts of suicide if they can't work soon.

Many fishermen lack a high school education and struggle with what they'll do if the oil is stopped but they can't fish, Carbo says.

"They want to believe it's going to work out," he says. "But there's a sense of, 'What's going to happen now?'"

Sal Sunseri says he is optimistic the Gulf can recover. It has been painful, though, to see his 134-year-old New Orleans [Louisiana] family business, P&J Oyster Company, lose 70% of its sales and lay off 10 of 19 employees.

"My whole life has been turned around," Sunseri says.

Oyster fishermen show some of the highest anxiety, Carbo says. Two freshwater diversions opened off the Mississippi River to repel the oil have killed off hundreds of young oysters, throwing future harvests into doubt.

Dave Casanova, a Shell Beach [Louisiana] oysterman, says nearly two-thirds of his young oysters have died, pushing his earnings back two or three years. The mental strain of having to support a wife, four daughters and two grandchildren has been draining.

Casanova, 54, says he saves his BP pay for the day the company pulls out and the fishermen are left with dead oyster beds. He says he hopes other fishermen are doing so.

"The full effect of this spill is going to be felt much, much later."

—Rick Jervis

For teenagers who face this kind of torment, every school day is miserable. After facing hardship day after day for a long time, the stress builds up to the point at which some young people become clinically depressed. "I hated going to school because of what the other kids would say," says Sharon. "My sister was so popular and pretty and there I was, all ugly and fat. The other kids always teased me, especially in gym class. I hated myself."

Once depression sets in, it changes the way a person thinks. It alters and distorts reality. Life tends to begin to look gloomy and dull, and the future appears darker. Negative thoughts and pessimism creep in to make it seem that things are bound to go wrong. Feelings of helplessness tend to take over and make it seem pointless to try to change things for the better. Self-confidence and self-esteem seem to vanish, and self-blame tends to emerge. It is difficult to remember feeling happy, and it seems impossible to feel hopeful that joy will ever be felt again.

What does all of this add up to for teenagers? Some end up developing self-destructive behavior, such as lying, stealing, fighting, cutting class, running away from home, using drugs and alcohol, becoming sexually promiscuous, or engaging in self-cutting. And some attempt or follow through with suicide.

COEXISTING CONDITIONS

It is the rule rather than the exception that depression exists in conjunction with one or more other disorders. These include anxiety disorders, conduct disorder, oppositional defiant disorder, attention deficit/hyperactivity disorder (ADHD), learning disabilities, eating disorders, and drug and alcohol abuse. When another condition coexists with depression, both must be treated, which makes management of the disorder more difficult.

ANXIETY DISORDERS

Some of the anxiety disorders that affect teenagers include separation anxiety disorder, generalized anxiety disorder, obsessive-compulsive disorder (OCD), phobias, and post-traumatic stress disorder (PTSD). These conditions usually coexist with major depression. Feeling homesick when away from home, worrying about the well-being of parents, and avoiding going to school are some of the signs of separation anxiety disorder.

A sign of generalized anxiety disorder can include excessively worrying about future events (an upcoming test, for example) as well as past events, usually with feelings of guilt. Young people with this disorder tend to be perfectionists and to care a great deal about what others think of them. They often appear anxious and nervous, engaging in foot tapping or nail-biting, for example. They also tend to be irritable and to become tired easily.

Obsessive-compulsive disorder is characterized by an obsession, which is a persistent thought or impulse to do something, and a compulsion, which is a repetitive behavior. Individuals with OCD experience the thought or impulse and then feel forced to act on it. For example, a person may be obsessed with thoughts about coming into contact with germs. As a result, he or she may feel compelled to wash his or her hands over and over again in an attempt to rid them of germs. "My problem was feeling like I had to have the bottom sheet on my bed wrinkle-free before I could fall asleep," says Jordynn. "I hated having to keep getting up and straightening it. I would get so tired doing that—I didn't want to do it, but I just couldn't help myself."

Phobias are intense and irrational fears of ordinary objects or activities, such as excessive fear of heights or enclosed spaces. Some young people suffer from social phobias, such as an excessive fear of speaking in front of the class or eating in front of other people.

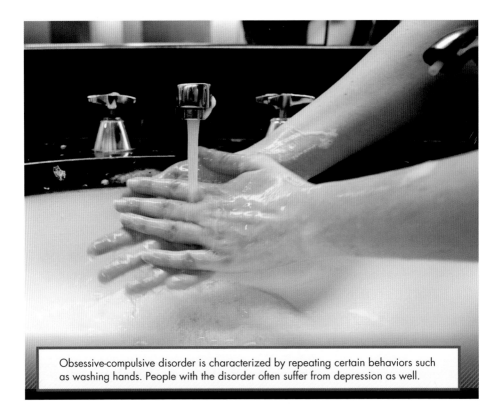

Obsessive-compulsive disorder is characterized by repeating certain behaviors such as washing hands. People with the disorder often suffer from depression as well.

Post-traumatic stress disorder can result from experiencing an event that is shocking and unanticipated and is beyond what usually occurs in a person's life. Examples include physical and sexual abuse, rape, kidnapping, and threatened death. When these events happen in a person's life, the trauma can be so severe that the individual may be left with intense feelings of fear and helplessness.

Symptoms of PTSD include recurrent and distressing memories or dreams of the event and feeling as if the traumatic event were happening all over again. People suffering from PTSD may feel detached from familiar activities, be irritable and anxious, and experience problems with sleep and concentration. People who witness a trauma to another person or who learn about a trauma that has affected a close friend or family member may also suffer the onset of PTSD as a result.

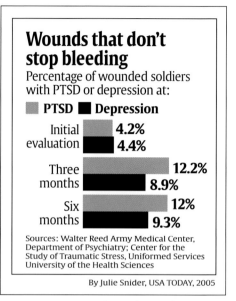

Wounds that don't stop bleeding
Percentage of wounded soldiers with PTSD or depression at:

	PTSD	Depression
Initial evaluation	4.2%	4.4%
Three months	12.2%	8.9%
Six months	12%	9.3%

Sources: Walter Reed Army Medical Center, Department of Psychiatry; Center for the Study of Traumatic Stress, Uniformed Services University of the Health Sciences

By Julie Snider, USA TODAY, 2005

CONDUCT DISORDER

Individuals who suffer from conduct disorder exhibit behavior that ignores the basic rights of other people and breaks the rules of society. They show no remorse for their actions. Many young people with conduct disorder are bullies. They tend to start fights and to be deliberately cruel to people or animals. They also tend to lie, steal, stay out late at night, run away from home, skip school, and intentionally destroy property. In addition, young people who suffer from conduct disorder often become involved in drug and alcohol use as well as sexual promiscuity. This disorder is more common in boys than girls, and it usually coexists with dysthymia.

OPPOSITIONAL DEFIANT DISORDER

Individuals who suffer from oppositional defiant disorder (ODD) exhibit a persistent pattern of negative, hostile, and defiant behavior that lasts for six months or longer. Many young people who are diagnosed with this disorder tend to argue and have angry outbursts at home. They are somewhat more obedient and in control of themselves in public places, including school. It is not unusual for young people with ODD to tease and torment siblings, provoke shouting matches with parents, and break rules just for spite.

Physical fighting may also erupt. Those with ODD are also notorious for blaming others for their problems. Some individuals with ODD go on to develop conduct disorder.

ATTENTION DEFICIT/HYPERACTIVITY DISORDER

Finding it difficult to stick with a task, sit still, be patient, and think before acting are all symptoms of ADHD. Young people with ADHD also tend to be disorganized, messy, and careless in doing schoolwork. Many are forgetful and often misplace their belongings.

LEARNING DISABILITIES

Young people who have learning disabilities have normal intelligence but have trouble with school achievement in reading, writing, speaking, listening, and/or doing mathematics. One of the most common learning disabilities is dyslexia, a language-

Teens with ADHD find it very challenging to focus. Many depressed teens also have ADHD.

communication disorder that causes difficulty with reading and comprehension.

EATING DISORDERS

Compulsive or binge eating, anorexia nervosa, and bulimia nervosa are eating disorders commonly associated with depression. Some individuals suffer from a blend of both anorexia and bulimia. These disorders tend to affect more females than males. Obesity can be the result of compulsive or binge eating (consuming large amounts of food in a short period of time). Those who suffer from this disorder become significantly overweight, putting their health in jeopardy.

Anorexia nervosa is a sharp decrease in the intake of food or refusal to eat at all. Although anorexics are often emaciated, they continue to see themselves as fat. Other symptoms include developing unusual eating habits, exercising obsessively, and a cessation of monthly menstrual periods due to low body weight.

Bulimia nervosa involves binge eating and then purging (getting rid of the food) by vomiting or by using laxatives to cause bowel movements. Consequently, large amounts of food are eaten without weight gain. Other symptoms include developing eating rituals, eating secretly, and spending long periods of time in the bathroom. Bulimics tend to suffer from low self-esteem and be overly concerned with the opinions of other people. Parents of bulimics tend to be achievement-oriented perfectionists. Their mothers tend to be extremely concerned about their own weight and appearance. "Once I started making myself vomit, I could eat as much as I wanted and not gain any more weight," says Sharon. "I used to hide food in my room and eat it at night without anyone knowing and then make myself throw up. I loved it and hated it all at the same time. I loved it because I could eat and not gain weight, but I hated it because I

People with depression often have issues with food, both overeating and undereating, which can lead to severe eating disorders such as anorexia and bulimia.

couldn't control what I was doing. I had gotten to the point where I had to do it that way. I couldn't eat normally anymore."

ALCOHOL AND DRUG ABUSE

Depression is a leading cause of alcoholism and drug abuse. Many individuals who suffer from depression are in such deep emotional pain that they look for relief. They turn to alcohol or drugs in an effort to escape sad or lonely feelings or to feel less anxious. In addition to alcohol and cigarettes, teenagers use marijuana, LSD, cocaine, and heroin. Some inhale the gas in aerosol cans of glue, paint, room deodorizers, and whipped cream to get high. Both alcohol and drugs do the job of numbing the pain and relieving feelings of anxiety—but these effects are only temporary. After the effects of these substances wear off, the depression returns and is usually worse.

Alcohol and marijuana are depressant drugs. The negative effects of substance abuse include memory loss, infections, lung disease, risk-taking behavior, accidents, school failure, and death. "I liked the feeling I got from smoking marijuana and drinking," says Doug. "When I was messed up, I forgot about my problems. Nothing bothered me. But afterward, the problems were still there. I guess that's why I kept smoking and drinking. I wanted to feel better after feeling so bad. It was a vicious cycle. It just added to my problems, though, because now I have to go to summer school to take the classes I failed."

CHAPTER THREE

DIAGNOSIS AND TREATMENT

JORDYNN'S STORY

Jordynn, an only child, had dreaded her mother's marriage to Peter. Jordynn's parents had been divorced for several years, but Jordynn's father lived only a short distance away and Jordynn saw him regularly. He assured her that he had positive feelings about the marriage and hoped she did as well. Jordynn liked her mother's new husband, but she was not happy about the marriage because it meant there was no chance of her mother and father ever getting back together. Jordynn also resented that she would have to share her mother with Peter every day. She worried that there would be no time for the two of them to do things together.

Jordynn had participated in her town's summer theater program before and had loved it, but this summer was different. She could not seem to become enthused about it. Her mother packed her a lunch every day, but Jordynn found that she had no appetite. She ended up throwing most of the food away and did not tell her mother. By the end of the summer, she had lost weight and her mother expressed concern.

"I told Jordynn that she looked thin, but she said it was from the dancing they were doing for the summer musical," says Jordynn's mother. "I didn't think too much about it because I thought her explanation made sense. Plus, it had been so hot all summer and I know it's hard to have much of an appetite when it's hot. I thought Jordynn was eating properly because I packed her lunch. I had no idea she was throwing it away."

When school started, Jordynn began to awaken very early in the morning and was unable to fall back to sleep. She would feel exhausted for the rest of the day, and she found it difficult to concentrate during her classes. She also found it difficult to get along with her friends. She had become so short-tempered with them that they started avoiding her. When she got home from school at the end of the day, all she wanted to do was be alone in her room. She would put on some music, lie across her bed, and stare at the ceiling. She had to be coaxed to the dinner table and then would pick at her food.

"My mom and Peter would ask me over and over again what was wrong," says Jordynn. "I wasn't really sure what was wrong. I knew I was upset about the marriage, but I was beginning to feel like my whole life was out of control. I couldn't feel happy about anything—not even the things that I knew were coming up during the school year, like dances and parties and all. And my friends had stopped calling me."

By late September, the field hockey season was a few weeks along. Jordynn had missed five practices because she was tired and felt unenthusiastic about playing. She also complained to her mother about stomachaches. On the day of the next practice, she told her mother that she was quitting the team.

"That really took me by surprise," says Jordynn's mother. "She had lost a lot of weight, seemed overly tired, complained of stomachaches, was not getting her homework finished, and now she wanted to quit hockey after happily playing for three years. I knew something was wrong. I was afraid she might have a serious illness, so I made an appointment with the pediatrician."

The pediatrician examined Jordynn and ordered some laboratory tests. He also asked Jordynn and her mother several questions. After finding nothing physically wrong with Jordynn, he recommended that she be evaluated by a psychiatrist experienced in dealing with teenagers.

The psychiatrist, Dr. Goldy, met with Jordynn and gave her several tests before talking to her and then her mother. During her discussion with Dr. Goldy, Jordynn confided to him that for a long time she had felt compelled to straighten the bottom sheet on her bed so that there were no wrinkles in it before she was able to fall asleep. Dr. Goldy concluded that Jordynn suffered from both depression and obsessive-compulsive disorder and recommended that she begin treatment with medication and psychotherapy.

"I met with Dr. Goldy every Tuesday," says Jordynn. "I found that I actually looked forward to Tuesdays because I knew I could talk about the things that were bothering me and that Dr. Goldy would help me work through them. And it felt good to be able to say exactly what was on my mind without hurting anyone's feelings. I could never really say everything to my mom or my dad because I didn't want to hurt them. I wanted to be careful not to say anything that would make them feel bad about the divorce or the remarriage. And I didn't want to hurt Peter, either. He is good for my mom and I'm glad she has him. I'm glad I have him, too. He would do anything for me and I know I'm really lucky. I don't know why the remarriage upset me so much, but it did. I wasn't able to find anything about my

Regular visits to a mental health professional are an important part of treatment for most types of depression.

life that made me happy, and when I looked ahead to the future, it was dark, too. Dr. Goldy helped me understand that the bad feelings I had were not my fault. He made me understand that depression is an illness. And we found out that my grandmother and my grandmother's aunt suffered from depression, so it runs in our family."

Jordynn is eating and sleeping normally now, and she feels happy. She is also enjoying her friends again and is looking forward to the special occasions that are coming up at school. She still meets with Dr. Goldy, although not as often. "There are things that upset me from time to time," says Jordynn. "Just knowing that Dr. Goldy is there to listen and give me guidance has helped me so much."

DIAGNOSIS

Doctors can diagnose some conditions with a blood test or X-ray. This is not so with depression. Diagnosing depression is a complex process. Health professionals must gather information from a variety of sources. Then a health professional experienced in diagnosing and treating depression has to analyze it.

Psychiatrists are medical doctors and can prescribe medication. Some psychiatrists provide psychotherapy, while others leave this to psychologists. Psychologists typically hold either a PhD (doctor of philosophy) or a PsyD (doctor of psychology) degree. They are not medical doctors. Psychiatrists and psychologists sometimes work together in diagnosing and treating a patient with depression.

A pediatrician, a family physician, a school psychologist, or a guidance counselor can recommend qualified mental health professionals who specialize in working with teenagers. Universities, hospitals, and medical centers have mental health professionals on staff. Many universities have a psychology department with an in-house clinic, and most medical schools and medical centers have private practice groups or clinics that deal with mental health.

More than one health professional may have to take part in the evaluation process since it is complex. The process should include a physical examination, patient history, psychological testing, and an interview with the teenager as well as with his or her parents or guardian. Because depression tends to affect so many aspects of a young person's life, the mental health professional who is making the diagnosis must find out about how the young person is functioning in all areas of his or her life.

PHYSICAL EXAMINATION

The symptoms of depression frequently involve physical discomfort (such as stomachaches, headaches, and fatigue) and changes in appetite. The pediatrician or family physician is often the first health professional parents turn to, as Jordynn's, Lindsay's, and Anthony's parents did. The doctor will do a thorough physical examination to determine whether there is another condition causing the symptoms. Diabetes, thyroid problems, and mononucleosis, a viral illness, for example, can be associated with stomach discomfort, weight changes, mood changes, or fatigue. The doctor may also order blood and urine laboratory tests and possibly an electrocardiogram, a test that checks the electrical activity of the heart, to gather as much information as possible. If the results of the physical examination and tests show no problems, and if the doctor suspects that depression exists, he or she will suggest consulting a mental health professional. The doctor can recommend psychiatrists and psychologists in the area who specialize in evaluating teenagers. The rest of the evaluation should be conducted by one of these mental health professionals.

PATIENT HISTORY

The psychiatrist or the psychologist will gather information from parents to find out about the teenager's history. This includes developmental information such as the age at which he or she began to crawl, walk, and talk and medical information, including any illnesses, accidents, and surgeries that have occurred since infancy. The doctor will ask about the adolescent's psychological background, including temperament and fears since early childhood, and educational history, including school performance and attention problems. The parents will also provide details about the teenager's family, including the relationship between the mother, the father, and other family members, as well as any mood or anxiety disorders, learning disabilities, or alcoholism in blood relatives.

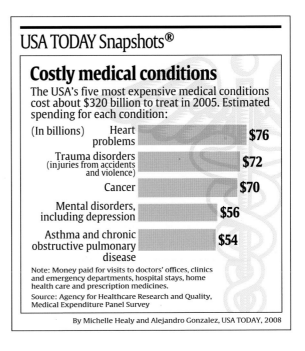

USA TODAY Snapshots®

Costly medical conditions

The USA's five most expensive medical conditions cost about $320 billion to treat in 2005. Estimated spending for each condition:

(In billions)

Condition	Amount
Heart problems	$76
Trauma disorders (injuries from accidents and violence)	$72
Cancer	$70
Mental disorders, including depression	$56
Asthma and chronic obstructive pulmonary disease	$54

Note: Money paid for visits to doctors' offices, clinics and emergency departments, hospital stays, home health care and prescription medicines.

Source: Agency for Healthcare Research and Quality, Medical Expenditure Panel Survey

By Michelle Healy and Alejandro Gonzalez, USA TODAY, 2008

PSYCHOLOGICAL TESTS

Mental health professionals use certain tests to assess an individual's intelligence and academic achievement. These tests can also assess attention span, impulsiveness, and self-esteem. Other tests reveal the person's self-image, social issues, or moodiness. Parents are asked to fill out questionnaires that address how the teenager behaves in various settings, such as home or school.

www.usatoday.com

USA TODAY

Life

SECTION D

June 3, 2009

From the Pages of USA TODAY

Depression, anxiety pass from parents to kids

Children of parents with anxiety disorders are up to seven times more likely than others to develop anxiety problems themselves, research shows, and children of depressed parents also are at high risk for becoming depressed.

Two new studies suggest that talking to therapists can break the cycle, reducing the risk of mental health problems in children and teens.

Both studies released this week focused on "cognitive behavior therapy," in which patients learn to reframe the way they think about upsetting events to avoid falling into a depressive spiral.

Adolescence could be the best time to try to prevent depression, because most depressed adults say their problems started in their teen years, says Judy Garber of Nashville's Vanderbilt University [in Tennessee], author of a study in today's *Journal of the American Medical Association*. About one in five teens experience depression by age 18.

Depressed children are more likely to have trouble in school and are at increased risk for suicide or substance abuse, Garber says.

Garber's study focused on high-risk teens whose parents had a history of depression. All 316 of the teens already had experienced depression in the past or had some symptoms of depression when the

INTERVIEWS

The psychiatrist or the psychologist will usually talk with the parents and sometimes the other children in the family before talking with the teenager. He or she will hear the family's perspective on what problems they are dealing with and will see what influences the family members have on the teenager. The psychiatrist or the psychologist will then meet with the teenager separately to hear his or her perspective. They will discuss specific symptoms during this meeting.

Before making a diagnosis, the psychiatrist or the psychologist study began. Half were randomly assigned to attend eight weekly group sessions with other teenagers.

After nine months, teens who attended group therapy were less likely to have had an episode of depression than teens who had their usual care but didn't receive therapy, the study shows. The prevention program didn't help at all, however, for teens whose parents were currently depressed, Garber says.

Children of depressed adults may feel adrift because their parents aren't able to give them the support and encouragement they need, says Bryan King, director of child and adolescent psychiatry at Seattle Children's Hospital [in Washington], who wasn't involved in the study.

In addition to a genetic predisposition to depression, children may inherit their parents' negative attitudes.

In a small study from Johns Hopkins Children's Center, researchers tried to help children who weren't yet having anxiety problems. All 40 of the children, ages 7 to 12, had parents with anxiety disorders.

Researchers offered half of youngsters and their parents an eight-week course of "cognitive behavioral therapy." In these hour-long sessions, parents learned how to recognize things they were doing that might make their children anxious—such as being overprotective or worrying out loud. Children also learned coping skills, according to the study, in the June issue of the *Journal of Consulting and Clinical Psychology*, released Monday.

After a year, none of the children in therapy had developed an anxiety disorder. But doctors diagnosed anxiety disorders in 30% of children in the comparison group, who were placed on a waiting list but didn't receive therapy during the clinical trial, says lead author Golda Ginsburg, a child psychologist.

Few insurers pay for cognitive behavioral therapy, but Ginsburg says she hopes her study will provide evidence that it's worth the investment.

— Liz Szabo

may want to speak with teachers or coaches to learn more about school performance and behavior. Teachers also usually have insight into how their students relate to classmates, which can be helpful. A therapist will meet with a patient and his or her family in various combinations before diagnosing a patient's problem.

After reviewing all the information gathered from the physical examination, patient history, psychological tests, and interviews, the psychiatrist or the psychologist will make a diagnosis. If depression exists, he or she will determine both the form of depression and its severity before recommending treatment options. In addition, he or she will determine whether another condition coexists with the depression.

COPING WITH THE DIAGNOSIS

Young people and their parents react in various ways to a diagnosis of depression. Some teenagers feel angry that a problem has actually been found. Others deny that a problem exists, doubting the psychiatrist's or psychologist's findings. Some are frightened and many feel ashamed, believing that people will think they are crazy.

Many parents go through these same emotions once their child has been diagnosed with depression. Some even feel guilty. They feel that they are responsible, either genetically or by the way they have raised their child, for causing the depression. "Once I found out that Jordynn was depressed, I realized that my mother had suffered from depression off and on through the years," says Jordynn's mother. "I never really thought about it when Jordynn was acting so strangely. When I was growing up, there were times my mother would sit for hours in a chair by the radiator and just look out the window, and there were times my mother's aunt would also sit for long periods without any activity. Thinking back on it, I'm sure they were depressed. But no one talked about it. Now that Jordynn has been diagnosed with depression, I feel somewhat responsible. She must have inherited the tendency from my side of the family."

Most teenagers and their parents feel relieved when a diagnosis is made and they learn that treatment is available. "When Dr. Goldy explained about depression to us and assured us that it was treatable, I felt relieved," says Jordynn. "I didn't want to believe that something was wrong with me, but my life was such a mess that I actually felt happy when he came up with a real reason for why things were so bad. I felt like things were finally going to get better."

New Treatment Guidelines for Depression

The American Psychiatric Association announced changes to its recommendations for depression treatment in 2010. The new guidelines focus on a more personalized approach to treatment for people with depression. Each person's treatment should be tailored to their specific needs, according to the severity of their symptoms. In general, doctors should assess the patient's condition and adjust treatment accordingly. Treatment should include a combination of therapies including medication, psychotherapy, and changes in behavior, such as diet and exercise. Doctors should also monitor patients who have had three prior episodes of depression or suffer from chronic illness over the long term, rather than just treating their current depressive episode. Other new recommendations include consideration of the following:

- Electroconvulsive therapy (shock therapy), for people who do not benefit from medication

- New treatments such as transcranial magnetic stimulation (electromagnetic stimulation of brain regions linked with depression) and vagus nerve stimulation (electric charges delivered to the vagus nerve, which links the brain to internal organs)

- Regular exercise, which has shown proven benefits to older people with depression and those with chronic medical problems

Depression causes young people to have trouble taking initiative, developing independence and self-confidence, and establishing their own identity. Even more pressing is the fact that depression can lead to violent behavior, including suicide. Consequently, it is important to get help as early as possible to prevent episodes from recurring and to foster normal development. With proper treatment, most young people who suffer from depression can get well.

TREATMENT

The most common treatment for depression is psychotherapy or a combination of psychotherapy and medication. Although many mental health professionals accept psychotherapy alone as a beneficial method of treatment, especially for less severe depression, they usually do not favor using medication without the support of psychotherapy. This is because medication will boost the levels of neurotransmitters and restore proper brain functioning, but will not solve the problems of coping with stress, feeling more self-confident, or forming friendships. The skills needed to overcome these problems can be learned in psychotherapy. As a result, for many young people who are mildly or moderately depressed, psychotherapy alone may alleviate the symptoms of depression without the use of medication. But those who are more severely depressed may also need medication.

PSYCHOTHERAPY

Psychotherapy is the treatment of a mental or emotional disorder by a professionally trained and licensed individual who uses a variety of techniques to improve the mental health and coping skills of a patient or group of patients. Psychotherapists can be psychologists, psychiatrists, counselors, or social workers. Psychotherapy is sometimes called talk therapy.

Through regular meetings (weekly or monthly, for example) with a trained mental health professional, depressed people learn how to make positive changes in their attitude, emotions, and behavior. Some feel better after just talking about their concerns, while others must actively find solutions to problems that contributed to the development of the depression. Some people must learn to express anger and hostility without becoming aggressive. In addition, psychotherapy helps people work through the relationship problems that accompany depression. Improving social skills can help in the recovery process and is important to general well-being.

Therapists use several types of psychotherapy in treating their patients. Research suggests that a combination of cognitive therapy and behavioral therapy, referred to as cognitive-behavioral therapy, is most effective in treating depression. Other effective types of psychotherapy doctors use to treat depression are interpersonal therapy, family therapy, and group therapy.

COGNITIVE-BEHAVIORAL THERAPY

Cognitive therapy focuses on helping to change negative and distorted views of the self, the world, and the future. It also helps people learn the skills necessary for dealing with emotions and relating to other people. Behavioral therapy focuses on changing specific problem behaviors by using rewards for desirable behavior and either no rewards or negative consequences for undesirable behavior. A combination of these two approaches helps the depressed person to view himself or herself and the world more positively and accurately, to get involved in pleasurable activities, and to interact successfully with other people.

INTERPERSONAL THERAPY

This therapy helps the depressed person identify and solve the current problems he or she is having with other people. For young people, these problems may include not being able to form friendships, being rejected by classmates, or arguing with parents. Interpersonal therapy teaches communication skills that help the depressed person successfully and confidently interact with other people. Whether the relationship problem triggers the depression or whether the depression causes the relationship problem, interpersonal therapy is designed to identify the nature of the problem and then find solutions.

FAMILY THERAPY

In addition to meeting alone with the depressed teenager, the therapist may also meet with the family. Family therapy not only helps all members of the family understand and cope with

Many doctors will recommend that depressed teens and their families attend family therapy. In these sessions, the family learns to address causes and effective ways to support the mental health of the depressed person.

depression, but it also investigates the possibility that the young person's depression stems from problems within the family. These include marital problems, lack of adequate guidance, no set limits, or absence of a parent through divorce or death. The therapist helps all family members learn to communicate more effectively with one another and teaches them ways to solve problems as they arise. "Therapy has helped us to be more in tune with Kevin's needs," says his mother. "My husband and I have learned to put less pressure on Kevin about school. We listen to him now and try to see things more from his perspective rather than only from our perspective as parents. We're trying not to play down the things that bother him. They are important to him at his age. We are learning to understand and respect that."

GROUP THERAPY

This type of therapy involves a therapist working with a group of clients. Family therapy can help a patient and his or her parents deal with the patient's depression and with any other problems within the family that may have contributed to the depression. Although some teenagers feel uncomfortable in a group setting with their peers, some actually feel more comfortable. By being part of a group, some depressed teenagers feel less isolated and alone, which are feelings typically associated with depression. In addition, many teenagers are often more willing to accept suggestions and solutions from their peers than from a doctor or a therapist. An added advantage of the group setting is that the participants take turns speaking, so a person speaks only when he or she wants to.

CHOOSING A THERAPIST

The therapist may be a psychiatrist, a psychologist, a social worker, or a psychiatric nurse. Many states also have certified counselors.

Group therapy is also a common treatment for depressed individuals. The group is often led by a mental health professional and allows depressed people to talk to others who are going through the same thing.

Counselors often have a specialization, such as family or marriage counseling. It is always best to choose someone who is licensed in his or her field. This indicates that the therapist has adequate training and experience in psychotherapy. In addition, licensed therapists are held to working within the professional standards of their profession, and they must keep abreast of changes and progress in their field by updating their education from time to time. The therapists who are most likely to meet with success in treating a depressed teenager are those who are warm and caring, who provide a trusting environment, and who put the depressed teenager and his or her family members at ease. The better the match between the teenager and the therapist, the more successful the treatment is likely to be. Research has shown that the single greatest factor in whether or not psychotherapy is successful is the comfort the teenager feels with his or her therapist.

MEDICATION

When depression is severe or has been long-lasting, the mental health professional may prescribe medication to be used in combination with psychotherapy. Only medical doctors are able to prescribe medication. Ideally, a psychiatrist experienced in treating depression in teenagers should decide what medication and dosage are best. Pediatricians and family doctors may also make this determination, but they are typically not trained in treating depression in teenagers.

The medications used for treating depression include a variety of antidepressants. Lithium is used for treating bipolar disorder. As the medication balances the levels of neurotransmitters in the brain, clearer and more accurate thinking becomes possible. This helps the individual receiving treatment to be more receptive to the emotional and behavioral changes that the therapist will strive for during psychotherapy.

Antidepressant medication comes in various types and works in different ways. Although they are sometimes thought of as mood elevators, they are really mood regulators. They simply restore the amounts of neurotransmitters in the brain to normal levels. Antidepressant medications are not "uppers," meaning that they have no mood-altering effect on individuals who are not depressed, and they are not addictive. Different antidepressant medications work to correct the amounts of neurotransmitters in the brain. Some slow down the breakdown (destruction) of neurotransmitters, while others prevent the reuptake (reabsorption) of neurotransmitters.

April 26, 2010

From the Pages of USA TODAY

Exercise vs. anxiety

Most people seeking treatment for depression or anxiety face two choices: medication or psychotherapy. But there's a third choice that is rarely prescribed, though it comes with few side effects, low costs and a list of added benefits, advocates say.

The treatment: exercise.

"It's become clear that this is a good intervention, particularly for mild to moderate depression," says Jasper Smits, a psychologist at Southern Methodist University in Dallas [Texas]. Exercise as an anxiety treatment is less well-studied but looks helpful, he says.

It's no secret that exercise often boosts mood: The runner's high is legendary, and walkers, bikers, dancers and swimmers report their share of bliss.

Now, data pooled from many small studies suggest that in people diagnosed with depression or anxiety, the immediate mood boost is followed by longer-term relief, similar to that offered by medication and talk therapy, says Daniel Landers, a professor emeritus in the department of kinesiology at Arizona State University.

Many people find that regular exercise such as running helps treat their depression in addition to keeping their physical body healthier.

And exercise seems to work better than relaxation, meditation, stress education and music therapy, Landers says.

"Most physicians and therapists are aware of the effects," says Chad Rethorst, a researcher at the University of Texas Southwestern Medical Center in Dallas. "But they may not be comfortable prescribing it."

Smits and another researcher, Michael Otto of Boston University [in Massachusetts], are on a mission to change that. The two have written a guidebook for mental-health professionals and are working on guides for primary care physicians and consumers.

Ideally, Smits says, depressed or anxious people would get written exercise prescriptions, complete with suggested "doses" and strategies for getting started and sticking with the program.

One thing that helps people keep up this therapy, he says, is the immediate boost that many report. The same can't be said of taking pills, he says.

Questions still to be answered

But Smits and other exercise-as-treatment enthusiasts are quick to say that medications and psychotherapy are good treatments, too, and can be combined with exercise. "They work well," Smits says. "But too few people get them, and few get them in the doses that are needed."

Many people who start talk therapy or medications soon stop using them because of costs, side effects, inconvenience or other factors. In short-term studies, at least as many people stick with exercise as with drugs, Rethorst says. Not known, he says, is "how this will translate into the real world."

Other remaining questions:

- What kind of exercise works? Most studies have focused on aerobic exercise, such as running and walking, but have not ruled out strength training or other regimens.

- How much is needed? At least one study shows results from the amount recommended for physical health: 150 minutes of moderate exercise (such as brisk walking) or 75 minutes of vigorous exercise (such as running) each week.

- How does it help? Does it boost certain brain chemicals? Induce deeper sleep? Give patients a sense of action and accomplishment?

- Can it prevent initial bouts or recurrences of depression and anxiety?

That seems likely, says Michelle Riba, a psychiatrist who works with cancer patients and others at the University of Michigan. She prescribes exercise to depressed patients as part of a long-term plan for healthier living that includes sleep, eating and, in many cases, weight loss. Exercise can be especially important, she says, for patients taking antidepressant medications that cause weight gain.

"I don't think exercise will ever be the only treatment, but it may be a major part of preventing recurrences," she says. "It should be part of everybody's plan of health."

—Kim Painter

The Facts about Depression and Its Treatment

Getting past the stigma associated with depression and seeking help is the first step toward recovery. The following are common myths about depression and the facts that dispute them:

Myth: Depression is not a real medical problem.
Fact: Research has proven that depression is a real and serious condition. The medical community acknowledges it as a disease.

Myth: Depression is something that strong people can "snap out of" by thinking positively.
Fact: No one chooses to be depressed. People with depression cannot just "snap out of" their condition any more than someone with diabetes can.

Myth: Depression will just go away on its own.
Fact: While depression sometimes goes away without treatment, this is not usually the case. Without treatment, symptoms of depression can continue for weeks, months, or even years.

Myth: Antidepressants will change your personality.
Fact: Antidepressants are designed to change only the chemicals in your brain that cause the symptoms of depression. They do not to change your personality, but can take the "edge" off and help people with depression to cope with daily life.

Source: Mental Health America, http://www.nmha.org/go/backtocampus/depression

And some increase the amount of neurotransmitters released from the sacs on the nerve endings. In each case, the result is the same—restoration of normal levels of neurotransmitters in the brain. Antidepressant medications can be grouped into three main categories: selective serotonin reuptake inhibitors (SSRIs), tricyclic antidepressants, and monoamine oxidase inhibitors (MAOIs).

SELECTIVE SEROTONIN REUPTAKE INHIBITORS

Fluoxetine (trademark: Prozac), sertraline (Zoloft), and paroxetine (Paxil) are drugs that prevent the reuptake of the neurotransmitter serotonin. Reuptake is the reabsorption of a neurotransmitter by the neuron that released it. This allows greater amounts to remain in the brain and restores the serotonin level to normal. SSRIs have few serious side effects and are the most commonly prescribed antidepressants. The side effects that seem to be associated with SSRIs are headaches and nausea. Researchers have found that Prozac can also help some young people who suffer from anxiety disorders and obsessive-compulsive disorder.

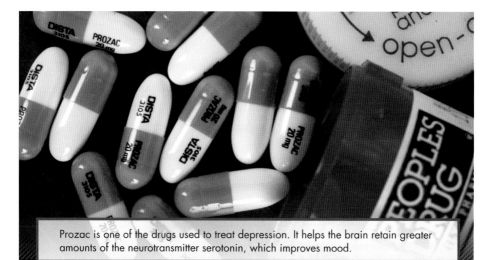

Prozac is one of the drugs used to treat depression. It helps the brain retain greater amounts of the neurotransmitter serotonin, which improves mood.

TRICYCLIC ANTIDEPRESSANTS

Tricyclic antidepressants, such as imipramine (Tofranil) and desipramine (Norpramin), are similar to SSRIs, but they raise the levels of norepinephrine as well as serotonin. Common side effects include dry mouth, constipation, and drowsiness. They sometimes cause increased heart rate, so people with heart conditions cannot take them.

MONOAMINE OXIDASE INHIBITORS

Monoamine oxidase is an enzyme (a protein produced in a cell) that is found in many parts of the body. In the brain, monoamine oxidase destroys, or breaks down, the neurotransmitters norepinephrine and serotonin. Monoamine oxidase inhibitors block the breakdown of the neurotransmitters. This allows greater amounts of these neurotransmitters to remain in the brain, restoring the levels to normal. Phenelzine (Nardil), tranylcypromine (Parnate), and isocarboxazid (Marplan) are MAOIs. Monoamine oxidase inhibitors are often prescribed for people who do not respond to the tricyclics.

One major drawback of these drugs is that when combining them with certain foods, beverages, and medications can cause a serious—and sometimes fatal—reaction to occur. Patients must avoid foods and beverages that contain large amounts of the amino acid tyramine, including aged cheese, processed meats (hot dogs, bologna, and pepperoni, for example), wine, and beer. They must also avoid certain drugs, including nasal decongestants and cough medicines. The foods and medicines can cause severely elevated blood pressure, chest pain, headache, and vomiting. Because many teenagers often have a hard time giving up foods such as pepperoni pizza and hot dogs, and because some drink wine or beer, doctors are reluctant to prescribe MAOIs for them.

LITHIUM

Doctors prescribe lithium to treat bipolar disorder, or manic depression. It is effective in treating both the manic and depressive episodes characteristic of this form of depression. Researchers are still trying to understand how lithium works. There is a fine line between just the right amount of lithium and too much lithium in the body. Too much lithium could be toxic, so doctors must carefully monitor individuals who take this drug. They also need to do regular blood tests to keep track of the lithium level in the body. Side effects include weight gain, stomach upset, and fatigue. If the patient also experiences hallucinations or delusions, the doctor may prescribe an antipsychotic medication in addition to the lithium to relieve these symptoms. "Lithium is working well for me," says Anthony. "It gives me the chance to have a normal life."

OTHER ANTIDEPRESSANTS

Researchers are always working to develop new medications for depression. Serotonin and norepinephrine reuptake inhibitors such as duloxetine (Cymbalta), venlafaxine (Effexor), and desvenlafaxine (Pristiq) treat depression by increasing the amounts of the neurotransmitters serotonin and norepinephrine, which help maintain mental balance. Bupropion is a norepinephrine and dopamine reuptake inhibitor. One form, called Wellbutrin, treats major depressive disorder and SAD. Some doctors prescribe bupropion (Zyban) to help people stop smoking. It can reduce cravings and other withdrawal effects. Trazodone (Desyrel) and mirtazapine (Remeron) are calming medications that patients take in the evening to help them sleep.

RESPONSE TO MEDICATION

Everyone responds differently to medication. What works for one person may not work for another. It is important to let a doctor decide whether the medication is effective or whether another one would be more effective. Many doctors find that a combination of medications works best. Antidepressant medication becomes effective gradually, and it must be taken continuously in order to work. It typically takes between four and six weeks before the medication becomes effective, and full relief of symptoms may take months. The doctor may have to try more than one medication before settling on the best one and the proper dosage. This may sometimes take several months. It is often difficult to be patient during this long wait. Some young people want to give up and just stop taking the medication, but staying with the medication can pay off.

Improvement in concentration, decision making, and coping with life's disappointments are just some of the positive results. Patients taking the proper medication can expect more normal appetite and sleep patterns. Perhaps the most welcome change is in getting along with other people. Because anxiety and irritability tend to fade when the levels of neurotransmitters in the brain are boosted, people who take medication find it easier to enjoy friends and family.

BRAIN THERAPY

In rare instances, depression is severe and a combination of psychotherapy and medication is not effective. In those cases, the doctor may prescribe brain therapy.

ELECTROCONVULSIVE THERAPY

Electroconvulsive therapy (ECT) involves passing an electrical current through the brain two or three times per week for six to twelve weeks. Doctors use sedatives and muscle relaxers so the patient feels no pain or discomfort during the treatments. ECT is sometimes used for treatment of suicidal patients whose lives are in immediate

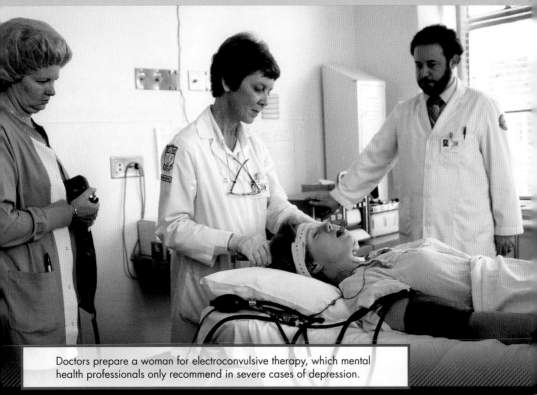

Doctors prepare a woman for electroconvulsive therapy, which mental health professionals only recommend in severe cases of depression.

danger. It is also an effective treatment for people on medications that interact poorly with antidepressants and for women who do not want to use drugs when they are pregnant. People who receive ECT are typically treated with psychotherapy and medication following the treatments.

OTHER BRAIN THERAPIES

Three new therapies for people who do not respond well to medication and psychotherapy are transcranial magnetic stimulation, vagus nerve stimulation, and deep brain stimulation. In transcranial magnetic stimulation, a doctor holds a large electromagnetic coil to the patient's scalp near the forehead. The coil sends painless electric currents that stimulate nerve cells in the region of the brain that controls mood. Scientists continue to study this treatment to

In vagus nerve stimulation therapy, a surgeon places this device, called a pulse generator, in the patient's chest. The implant sends electrical pulses into the brain.

determine its effectiveness and long-term side effects.

Vagus nerve stimulation (VNS) sends electrical impulses into the brain through the vagus nerve. There are two vagus nerves, one on each side of the body. Each nerve runs from the brain stem through the neck and down to the chest and the abdomen. In VNS a device called a pulse generator is surgically implanted in the chest. Wires, or leads, are attached to it and run under the skin to connect the generator to the left vagus nerve in the neck. (The right vagus nerve stimulates the heart, so VNS uses the left nerve to avoid cardiac complications.) Periodically, electrical signals pass along the vagus nerve to the mood centers of the brain. This can improve depression symptoms. Research into the effectiveness of this treatment is ongoing.

Deep brain stimulation is the most controversial brain therapy. The procedure began as a treatment for movement disorders such as Parkinson's disease, and the U.S. Food and Drug Administration has not yet approved its use for depression. The procedure is similar to VNS, but rather than wrapping wires around the vagus nerve, the surgeon places the leads directly in the brain. The leads are attached to the generator and run under the skin through the neck, behind

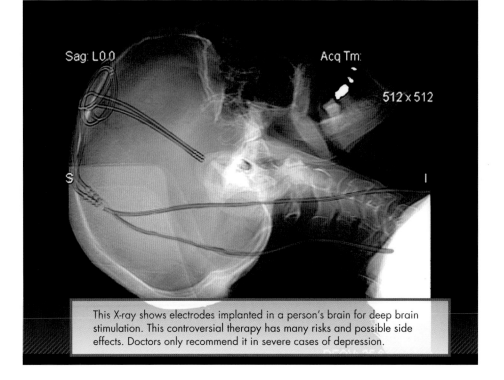

This X-ray shows electrodes implanted in a person's brain for deep brain stimulation. This controversial therapy has many risks and possible side effects. Doctors only recommend it in severe cases of depression.

the ear, and under the scalp. A small hole is then drilled in the skull where the lead enters the brain. Researchers continue to experiment with placement of the leads, as different regions show different results. Side effects of this procedure include bleeding, infection, and swelling. Improper lead placement can have negative cognitive and emotional side effects.

HOSPITALIZATION

When a depressed person has made a suicide attempt, when he or she has a definite plan for carrying out a suicide, or when he or she is threatening self-harm or harm to others, hospitalization may be necessary. People who lie in bed all day, stay up all night without being able to sleep, or dissolve into uncontrollable crying spells may also need hospitalization. Hospitalization can also help

Health-care providers sometimes recommend treatment at a hospital or a behavioral health facility like this one for people with depression.

people who abuse alcohol and drugs to get the help they need. Hospital settings are safe and controlled. As long as they are in the hospital, patients do not have to face the turmoil of family conflict, physical or sexual abuse, pressures at home or school, or pressures or humiliation by peers. Many welcome the routine of the hospital and the attention of the staff. The therapy included in the treatment plan usually focuses on helping people find ways to deal with stress and painful issues.

But hospitalization is not a positive experience for everyone. Some actually find it more stressful than their lives at home, and they feel greater despair and hopelessness as a result. Consequently, a doctor's decision to hospitalize a patient should be a carefully weighed decision. For teenagers who do not do well in a hospital setting, possible alternatives may include a foster home, a community group home, or the home of a relative or friend.

HOW LONG SHOULD TREATMENT CONTINUE?

The mental health professionals involved in the treatment determine its duration. This time varies from person to person. It can range from a few weeks to a lifetime, depending on the nature of the depression and its severity. For example, someone with mild depression may emerge from the depression after a few weekly psychotherapy sessions. Someone with bipolar disorder may need treatment with psychotherapy and medication for life. Research has shown that some people who receive treatment for depression overcome the depression and never need treatment again. Others overcome the depression but experience another episode at a later time. Still others require treatment on a long-term basis.

CHAPTER FOUR

SUICIDE AND ITS PREVENTION

uicide has strong ties to depression. Suicide is a response to feelings of loneliness, frustration, and helplessness. It is the third leading cause of death among teenagers in the United States. Only death by accident and homicide claim more teenage lives. And experts believe that some of the deaths that occur in accidents (such as car accidents) each year are really suicides. When a teenager is the only person in a car at the time of an accident and only that car is involved in the accident (such as when it hits a tree or a telephone pole), there is no way to know for certain whether the event was just an accident or whether the driver really meant to kill himself or herself.

Teenagers who attempt suicide typically display the following behaviors. There is no sure way to know in advance who will actually attempt suicide and who will not.

THE WARNING SIGNS OF SUICIDE

The following are signs typically associated with suicide:

- Experiencing a change in personality, such as becoming more downbeat and withdrawn or more irritable and explosive
- Suddenly becoming more upbeat and cheerful after being down for a long time
- Experiencing a drop in school performance
- Withdrawing from family, friends, or usual activities
- Neglecting personal appearance, such as not changing clothing from day to day or not combing hair
- Having accidents or engaging in risk-taking behavior, such as driving too fast, running away from home, or using drugs or alcohol

- Expressing strong feelings of worthlessness, such as "I'm no good" or "I'm a failure"
- Giving away or throwing away favorite possessions
- Being consumed by the theme of death in books and magazines, music, computer games, or on certain websites on the Internet

USA TODAY Snapshots®

How some teens registered despair

Percentage of high school students who say they felt so hopeless that they made a suicide plan in the past year:

Male
14.1%

Female
18.9%

Source: 2003 Youth Risk Behavior Survey, Centers for Disease Control and Prevention

By Cristina Abello and Sam Ward, USA TODAY, 2005

- Talking about life not being worth living or mentioning that he or she will not be a problem to anyone much longer. Some people actually say they are going to kill themselves. No mention of suicide should ever be taken lightly. Most teens who attempt suicide have spoken of their intention beforehand.
- Gathering guns, ropes, or other tools that can be used in carrying out a suicide
- Making prior suicide attempts

DEPRESSION AND SUICIDE

Depression is the single greatest risk factor for suicide. Two-thirds of all suicides are directly related to depression. Approximately 15 percent of the people who are depressed commit suicide as a result

www.usatoday.com

News
SECTION A

July 16, 2010

From the Pages of USA TODAY

June was worst month on record for Army suicides

Soldiers killed themselves at the rate of one per day in June making it the worst month on record for Army suicides, the service said Thursday.

There were 32 confirmed or suspected suicides among soldiers in June, including 21 among active-duty troops and 11 among National Guard or Reserve forces, according to Army statistics.

Seven soldiers killed themselves while in combat in Iraq or Afghanistan in June, according to the statistics. Of the total suicides, 22 soldiers had been in combat, including 10 who had deployed two to four times.

"The hypothesis is the same that many have heard me say before: continued stress on the force," said Army Col. Christopher Philbrick, director of the Army Suicide Prevention Task Force. He pointed out that the Army has been fighting for nine years in Iraq and Afghanistan.

Last year was the Army's worst for suicides with 244 confirmed or suspected cases.

The increase was a setback for the service, which has been pushing troops to seek counseling. Through May of this year, the Army had seen a decline in suicides among active-duty soldiers this year compared with the same period in 2009.

Philbrick expressed frustration over

of their depression. Although not every person who suffers from depression attempts suicide, most suicide attempts and completed suicides are carried out by people suffering from depression. Along with the rate of depression, the rates of both completed suicides and suicide attempts are on the rise. Thousands of teenagers commit suicide each year and thousands more try. Among teenagers, girls outnumber boys in attempted suicides, but boys outnumber girls in completed suicides. This is because girls are more likely to choose drug overdose (from which some can be saved), while boys are more the June deaths. "Because we believe that the programs, policies, procedures . . . are having a positive impact across the entire force. The help is there."

A leading military suicide researcher says changing a culture that views psychological illness as a weakness takes time.

"I would expect it to be years," said David Rudd, dean of the College of Social and Behavioral Science at the University of Utah in Salt Lake City.

The mounting stress on an Army facing renewed deployments and combat in Afghanistan is also a factor, Rudd said. "That's not a challenge they [Army leaders] control. It's a challenge that the president and Congress controls," he said.

The Army also unveiled on Thursday a training video designed to combat suicides. It contains testimonials by soldiers who struggled with self-destructive impulses before seeking help. It is titled *Shoulder to Shoulder: I Will Never Quit on Life.*

Philbrick said this was an improved video that he hoped would reach troubled soldiers. The previous video did not resonate with average soldiers, he said. During a showing in Baghdad [Iraq], soldiers laughed at it, Philbrick said. "In grunt language, it sucked," he said.

The Army's current suicide rate is about 22 deaths per 100,000, which is above a civilian rate that has been adjusted to match the demographics of the Army. That rate is 18-per-100,000. Only the Marine Corps has a higher suicide rate, at 24-per-100,000. Although Marine Corps suicides had been tracking similarly to last year's record pace, the service reported only one suicide in June.

Just among Guard and Reserve soldiers, suicides have occurred at a higher rate this year than last year, according to Army figures. There have been 65 confirmed or suspected cases this year, compared with 42 for the same period last year.

—Gregg Zoroya

likely to choose more violent and final methods, such as gunfire, jumping from a height, or hanging. Older teenagers are more likely than younger teenagers to complete a suicide.

Although some teenagers commit suicide on an impulse, most speak about their suicidal thoughts or at least give clues before an attempt. Any mention of suicide should be taken seriously. Although not every teenager who mentions suicide goes through with the act, most who do take their own lives have spoken about their feelings or intentions with someone else. Of the individuals who have carried out a suicide or a suicide attempt, many spent time thinking through how they would do it and devised a plan.

RISK FACTORS FOR SUICIDAL BEHAVIOR

Although not all depressed teenagers turn to suicide, some feel that suicide is the only way to end the pain they are suffering. There are many factors that increase the likelihood of a teenager turning to suicide.

- Having a family history of suicide
- Making a previous suicide attempt
- Suffering from disorders that affect emotions and behavior
- Experiencing stressful life events
- Moving to a new community or being abandoned by a boyfriend or a girlfriend
- Living with family conflict
- Being rejected
- Using drugs and alcohol
- Having poor peer relationships
- Having guns in the home
- Experiencing problems with sexual issues
- Experiencing school failure
- Being a perfectionist
- Being impulsive
- Having hallucinations or delusions

Suicide tends to run in families. Teenagers who have a close relative, especially a parent, who has committed suicide are more likely to attempt suicide. Scientists believe that genetic abnormalities in the way brain chemicals are produced and used explain part of the reason some individuals engage in suicidal behavior. But since teenagers who have lost a parent are more likely to become depressed and since depression can lead to suicide, experts believe that suicidal behavior probably results from a combination of both heredity and life events.

Many teenagers who have attempted suicide in the past attempt it again. Although the previous attempt or attempts may not seem serious, they are. The next attempt may be fatal.

Young people who steal, have uncontrollable rage, or engage in dangerous behavior are at greater risk for suicide. Some parents react to their child's negative behavior with disgust and rejection. Many teenagers take this to mean that their parents feel they would be better off without them. Suicide can be the result.

Traumatic events, such as losing a parent (through death, divorce, or abandonment) or being physically or sexually abused, can create enough stress to push vulnerable young people to consider suicide. "I felt that I had lost both my parents," says Molly. "After my mom died in the car accident, my dad just shut down. He was there in body, but that's it. He didn't interact with my sisters, brother, and me at all. So not only did I have to deal with my mom's death, but I had to cope with my dad's emotional withdrawal and all the work around the

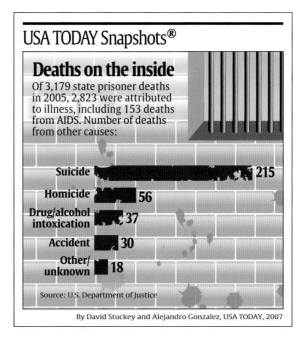

USA TODAY Snapshots®

Deaths on the inside

Of 3,179 state prisoner deaths in 2005, 2,823 were attributed to illness, including 153 deaths from AIDS. Number of deaths from other causes:

Suicide	215
Homicide	56
Drug/alcohol intoxication	37
Accident	30
Other/unknown	18

Source: U.S. Department of Justice

By David Stuckey and Alejandro Gonzalez, USA TODAY, 2007

house, plus taking care of my younger sisters and brother. And I had my schoolwork to keep up with, too. It all got to be too much. I just couldn't handle everything anymore. I had to find a way to end it and, at that time, the only way I could see to do that was to end my life."

Some individuals use a suicide attempt to try to get attention or sympathy from a specific person (such as a parent or a boyfriend or a girlfriend). Or they may be trying to punish this person for something hurtful they have done.

Teenagers who live in households where there is arguing or poor communication among family members, where a parent abuses alcohol or drugs, or where parents are preoccupied with their own lives tend to face a greater risk of suicide. Households that are made up of stepparents and step-siblings are often filled with conflict. And when teenagers try to discuss hopeless or suicidal feelings and parents either ignore them or play down the importance of what they are saying, teenagers are likely to feel even more frustrated and alone. This can increase the risk of suicide.

Teenagers tend to be extraordinarily sensitive to humiliation and rejection. When those who are at risk for committing suicide are faced with experiences that cause them to feel put down or rejected by others, suicide or a suicide attempt is sometimes the outcome. Events that tend to cause teenagers to feel this way include being teased by classmates, having a major argument with parents, being abandoned by a boyfriend or a girlfriend, not being chosen as a member of a team or organization, being disciplined at school, and facing problems related to sex and sexuality.

Teenagers who attempt or complete suicide often drink or use drugs just before carrying out the act. Alcohol and drugs tend to make people feel more uninhibited, often increasing feelings of anger and aggression or prompting more risk taking and self-destructive behavior.

In addition, alcohol is a depressant. Although it creates an initial feeling of well-being, it can lead to deeper feelings of depression.

Depressed teenagers tend to have greater difficulty forming and keeping friendships, and many isolate themselves from their peers. As a result, depressed teenagers tend to lack a support system when times are particularly tough. Not having a group of caring friends to turn to when life events are painful can add to a young person's despair.

Bullying can take on many forms, from physical harm to constant teasing to cyberbullying. Bullying can separate vulnerable teens from their peers and push them toward depression and suicidal thoughts.

For some, suicide seems like the only way to end the suffering. Additionally, depressed teenagers are sometimes drawn to others who also have problems, either personally or within their families. It is not unusual for these teenagers to support negative and dangerous behavior in one another.

Young people who commit suicide often do it on impulse. Having access to guns, either in their own homes or in friends' homes, can make killing themselves all the easier.

Sexual activity and issues of sexual identity can have a great impact on young people. Sexually transmitted diseases and unwanted pregnancies are some of the problems that can arise. But often the greatest anguish related to issues of sex and sexuality is among gay and lesbian teenagers. Their struggle to come to terms with what they are feeling and to gain acceptance by others often causes overwhelming despair leading to suicide.

Some teenagers who are competitive cannot tolerate any failure at school. For them, even minor academic failures or disappointments are intolerable. For others, learning disabilities stand in the way of academic achievement and can lead to criticism from teachers and teasing from classmates. Still others consider it a personal crisis when they face disciplinary action, such as getting detention or being suspended from school.

Teenagers who demand perfection from themselves may turn to suicide when facing disappointments such as losing in competition, not getting into a certain college, or not gaining acceptance by an organization, a club, or a team.

Teenagers who tend to react impulsively may turn to suicide as a spur-of-the moment response to a problem. This may occur even when the problem is minor, such as having an argument with a friend or facing a disappointment in sports, for example.

Hearing voices or seeing visions that are not real or having thoughts that are irrational can lead to suicidal behavior in some teenagers. For some, the voices actually tell them to kill themselves.

HOW DOES SUICIDE AFFECT FAMILY AND FRIENDS?

When a teenager commits suicide, family and friends are left with deep feelings of grief, anger, and confusion. It can be very difficult for them to come to terms with why such an act has taken place. Most

Death is always difficult for families. But when the death is the result of suicide, it can be even more difficult to come to terms with the loss of a loved one.

feel extremely guilty about not having been able to prevent such a tragedy. Many feel remorse over unresolved issues. Many also feel that the suicide victim has let them down.

When a young person makes a suicide attempt but does not die, it is common for family and friends to blame themselves for the attempt. Others feel angry, believing that the teenager could have chosen a different solution. Some feel ashamed. They feel that the suicide attempt reflects poorly on the family. And most feel scared. They wonder when and if another attempt will be made. "Ever since Molly took the pills, I've felt afraid that she'll do it again," says Molly's sister. "I feel better knowing she's in therapy."

USA TODAY

WHAT CAN BE DONE WHEN A TEENAGER IS SUICIDAL?

Anyone who shows the warning signs of suicide needs immediate professional help. To wait and see if things improve can have disastrous consequences. In fact, many suicides take place at home while other family members are also at home. If the individual who is showing suicidal tendencies is already in therapy, a family member should contact the therapist immediately. If not, an appointment should be made to see a mental health professional the same day. If there seems to be immediate danger of the young person harming himself or herself or others, a call should be placed to emergency services (9–1–1). In general, teenagers who are at risk for suicide need a caring person to show concern for their well-being. They need other people to be open and direct with them. It is best to ask a troubled teenager directly about any suicide plans he or she has made. Experts have learned that talking about a suicide does not put ideas in a young person's head. If he or she is suicidal, the thoughts are already there. The benefit of asking a teenager about his or her suicidal feelings is that he or she is likely to feel relieved that someone cares. He or she may feel more open to discussing the problem and finding alternatives to suicide.

Parents or other significant adults in the teenager's life (a favorite teacher, a compassionate neighbor, a minister, a priest, or a rabbi) should emphasize that they strongly believe suicide is wrong. Many mental health professionals recommend that adults get right to the point and say something like, "Suicide is unacceptable and is not an option." It is important for adults to assure the young person that they care about his or her safety. The following are additional ways that a parent or other caring adult can help a teenager who has considered suicide:

- Encourage a discussion of the struggles or disappointments that cause the despair

- Help find other possible ways to solve the problem
- Share stories of struggles or frustrations the adult faced as a teenager
- Make it clear that suicide is a permanent solution to a temporary problem
- Express the loss that the adult would feel if the young person were gone, and point out that the teenager would leave the survivors to deal with the pain

CRISIS COUNSELING

THERE IS HOPE
MAKE THE CALL

THE CONSEQUENCES OF JUMPING FROM THIS BRIDGE ARE FATAL AND TRAGIC.

This sign is posted on the Golden Gate Bridge in San Francisco, California, where many suicides occur. Call centers operate throughout the United States to give people considering suicide a place to talk about their problems.

www.usatoday.com
USA TODAY
Life
SECTION D

March 31, 2010

From the Pages of USA TODAY

A suicide prevention message to teenagers: 'We Can Help Us'

A public service ad campaign launching today is designed to help troubled teenagers before it's too late.

Suicide is the third leading cause of death among 15- to 24-year-olds, following accidents and homicides, according to government data.

In an effort to reduce such tragedies, the government worked with the Ad Council and the Inspire USA Foundation to create "We Can Help Us," a national public service advertising campaign. It includes TV, radio and print PSAs [public service announcements] as well as posters in schools and malls.

This campaign comes on the heels of a number of recent Associated Press reports of teen suicide:

- Phoebe Prince, 15, of South Hadley, Mass, hanged herself at home in January after experiencing a wave of severe taunting, bullying and physical threats by some fellow students in school and on Facebook.
- Marie Osmond's son Michael Blosil, 18, committed suicide in late February, jumping from the eighth floor of his apartment building in Los Angeles. He left a note in which he referred to his life-long battle with depression.
- Two sophomores from Norwood, Pa., died in an apparent suicide pact in February when they stood on train tracks and were killed by a high-speed Acela train.
- Six confirmed or suspected suicides have occurred this academic year at Cornell University in Ithaca, N.Y.

The public service campaign will offer help and direction, its sponsors say.

"Our goal with this national multimedia campaign is to provide support and resources for teens who are experiencing mental health problems," says Kathryn Power of the Substance Abuse and Mental Health Services Administration, part of the Department of Health and Human Services.

The aim is to help teenagers cope with very normal feelings of stress, loss and confusion, she says.

"Ultimately, our goal is to reduce the incidence of suicide and suicide attempts among teenagers, especially those between the ages of 13 to 17 who may be particularly vulnerable."

The ads urge young people to visit reachout.com, where they can watch videos of other teens who have had similar struggles. It emphasizes the National Suicide Prevention Lifeline (800-273-8255).

—*Nanci Hellmich*

time of change for young people as well as their parents. Although teenagers still rely on their parents for guidance, they feel the need to become more independent. Parents, meanwhile, try to adjust to this change. Many families pass through this period of transition smoothly. But sometimes problems seep into family life and create chaos. Depression can weaken the fibers of the family unit, and if left untreated, it can cause the family unit to fall apart.

Parents can sometimes react to their children in ways that injure their children's self-esteem. This can lead to depression in young people. Some parents are overly critical of their children and focus on their children's weaknesses rather than their strengths. Others are so preoccupied with their own lives or problems that they do not pay attention to their children's needs. They may also neglect to provide guidance. Some adults physically or sexually abuse the children in their households. Others are absent from the home as a result of divorce, business travel, or military assignment, which often creates a deep sense of loss in their children.

When a parent is depressed, family relationships and communication become especially strained. Many depressed parents are irritable and impatient when dealing with their children. Some are cold and withdrawn, withholding affection and neglecting their children's needs. Others, like Molly's father, are crippled by the symptoms of depression and cannot participate in family life. Their sad mood and fatigue may make it impossible for them to take part in family activities, help their children develop friendships, or set guidelines for them.

In some cases, the child must take on a parental role. This is what happened to Molly as a result of her mother's death and her father's resulting depression. Even though they strive for independence, teenagers still need to rely on their parents from time to time. When a teenager is the caretaker of a parent and other family members, the stress can be overwhelming.

It is not unusual for children of a depressed parent to develop depression themselves, partly because of the hereditary nature of depression and partly because of the everyday stress they must endure at home. Many feel guilty or responsible that their parent is depressed. Others try to protect the parent by holding their own feelings inside. Some resort to negative behavior in an effort to get the parent to show a response, or they act out with rebellion against the parent's problem.

Depressed teenagers and their parents (including stepparents) and siblings tend to argue frequently and intensely. Communication is likely to suffer, with parents and the teenager interrupting, criticizing, and ignoring one another. Discipline and punishment seem to be constant, and punishments tend to become harsher as parents become more and more exasperated.

HOW A TEENAGER'S DEPRESSION AFFECTS PARENTS

Parents go through a range of emotions when their son or daughter is depressed. Some see the teenager as either lazy or out of control and believe that the behavior is by choice. They often feel angry or irritated by their child's behavior. Others feel ashamed when their teenager has angry outbursts in front of other people, such as grandparents or family friends who come to visit. Many feel confused about why their child has so many problems, and they worry about what the future holds. Some feel guilty about their child's problems and blame themselves for being bad parents. Most feel deep pain over the feelings of worthlessness and despair that their teenager is suffering.

It is not unusual for depressed young people to be able to control themselves in public settings such as school, only to fall apart at home. Mornings and evenings tend to be difficult times. Waking up in a foul mood and taking too long to get ready for school usually causes an argument with parents. And avoiding homework in the evening can lead to anger and frustration. Teenagers who suffer from depression may complain a lot and pick fights with their brothers or sisters.

At the other end of the spectrum are the teenagers who totally withdraw from their family members. Upon returning home from school, they may go directly to their rooms. If they come to the dinner table, they are likely to be in a sullen mood and may sit silently through the meal. Others may skip dinner altogether. When the home environment is permeated by constant conflict, parents are likely to have trouble coping.

HOW A TEENAGER'S DEPRESSION AFFECTS SIBLINGS

The siblings of depressed teenagers often suffer. Many do not know enough about depression to understand what's wrong. Some worry that they somehow caused their brother or sister to become depressed. Others feel resentful of the extra time and attention their parents have to devote to the depressed sibling. Still others worry that they, too, may become depressed. And there are some young people who are embarrassed by the sad, withdrawn behavior their brother displays or afraid when their sister explodes in rage. Arguing among brothers and sisters is nothing unusual. But research shows that depressed young people tend to tangle with their siblings more often than those who are not depressed.

HOW A TEENAGER'S DEPRESSION AFFECTS FRIENDS

The symptoms of depression tend to interfere with a teenager's ability to make and keep friends. Peers are not likely to respond favorably to a teenager who does not want to participate in activities and has difficulty concentrating and remembering things. When depressed teenagers continually express negative feelings such as "Nothing ever works out right for me" or "I'm a failure" or "There's no use in even trying," their peers are likely to keep their distance.

www.usatoday.com

USA TODAY

Life

SECTION D

August 3, 2010

From the Pages of USA TODAY

Having a sister is healthy, study finds

Sisters can fend off ex-boyfriends, mean gossip and, apparently, depression.

Having a sister protects teens "from feeling lonely, unloved, guilty, self-conscious and fearful," according to a study in Monday's *Journal of Family Psychology*. Researchers from Brigham Young University [in Utah] in 2007 and 2008 studied 395 Seattle [Washington] families with two or more children. At least one child in each family was age 10 to 14.

They found that affectionate siblings have positive influences on each other no matter their age, gender or how many years they are apart. They promote behaviors such as kindness and generosity and protect against delinquency and depression, says Laura Padilla-Walker, assistant professor in Brigham Young University's School of Family Life.

And having a sister, rather than a brother, prevents depression, maybe because girls are better at talking about problems or are more likely to take on a caregiver role, Padilla-Walker says.

The study also found that siblings have twice as much influence as parents over performing good deeds—including volunteering, doing favors for others and being nice to people. "Siblings matter even more than parents do in terms of promoting being kind and generous," she says.

But brothers and sisters who exhibit hostility to each other are more likely to show aggressive behaviors in other relationships, says James Harper, Brigham Young University professor in the School of Family Life.

"Siblings are people that a child lives with every day, and yet we haven't really seriously considered their influence," he says.

The researchers say sibling influence was stronger in families with two parents than one. A child with a single parent may become a "parent figure" to a younger sibling, Padilla-Walker says.

—Stephanie Steinberg

Studies have found that having a sister decreases the risk of depression.

Some depressed teenagers are also argumentative and explosive. The result is that depressed young people end up with fewer and fewer friends, and some end up with no friends at all.

Getting dates and maintaining relationships with boyfriends or girlfriends is difficult for many of these young people, which further undermines their self-esteem. Particularly painful is having a boyfriend or a girlfriend break off an established relationship. As Kevin found, the feelings of failure, rejection, and worthlessness can become unbearable.

Some depressed teenagers end up in just the opposite situation. They maintain an extremely close relationship with one friend or with a group of friends. Many times these friends also suffer from depression or other problems with emotions and behavior. The problems they share seem to pull these young people together. They feel a strong desire to spend as much time as possible with one another, often shutting out family and other people. "Once I started hanging out with my older friends, I wanted to spend all my time with them," says Doug. "I liked being around them and I liked getting high. I didn't want to be at home with my family. At that time, I felt closer with my friends than with anybody in my family."

DEPRESSION AND SCHOOL

Teenagers who suffer from depression are likely to struggle academically. The symptoms of sadness, hopelessness, fatigue, poor concentration, difficulty remembering, and lack of enthusiasm for participating in activities tend to cause problems with school performance. For many, having difficulty sleeping and eating and the physical pain of stomachaches or headaches make doing well in school even more difficult. If other problems coexist with the depression, such as learning disabilities or attention deficit disorder, the situation becomes worse. Many teenagers who have these problems are teased by classmates and called "stupid" because of their poor school performance. Others fall into disruptive behavior as their frustration over difficulty with schoolwork increases. The result is likely to be punishment from teachers. As the self-esteem of these young people plummets, the feelings of failure, frustration, and hopelessness increase. Many skip class to avoid further embarrassment and failure, and some even drop out of school.

Since many depressed teenagers struggle socially at school, it is not uncommon for them to be criticized, shunned, or teased by their classmates. Since they are extraordinarily sensitive to criticism and failure, the rejection and humiliation can cause extreme pain. This intensifies the feelings of worthlessness, hopelessness, and anger. This pain sometimes leads to acts of violence.

SCHOOL BEHAVIOR THAT SIGNALS DEPRESSION

Many of the symptoms of depression are more easily recognized at home than at school (eating and sleeping problems or frequent bouts of crying, for example). Teachers and other school personnel may not always be aware of which students suffer from depression. But there are some signs, such as:

- Complaining of being bored in a class that used to be enjoyable
- Lacking energy or falling asleep in class (this may also signal alcohol or drug use)
- Frequently requesting to see the school nurse for headaches, stomachaches, or other pains
- Expressing feelings of not being able to do anything right or feeling "stupid"
- Misbehaving in class and expecting to be punished
- Arguing with the teacher and fighting with classmates
- Experiencing peer problems, such as withdrawing from or

becoming easily irritated by friends, or being shunned or teased by classmates
- Being unable to cope with frustration, such as angrily exploding after making mistakes
- Forgetting what has been learned or failing to finish assignments
- Talking or writing about death

WHAT PARENTS AND TEACHERS CAN DO TO HELP

In addition to treatment with psychotherapy or a combination of psychotherapy and medication, parents and teachers can take measures to improve the well-being of depressed teenagers. When parents are not present in the home or are not able to nurture their son or daughter, other significant adults in the teenager's life can give support. A grandparent, an aunt, an uncle, a family friend, a neighbor, a fellow church or a synagogue member, a sports coach, or a friend's parent can often fill in for a parent who is unable to help. These adults can do the following:

- Make time for discussing the day's events, sharing feelings, and taking part in an activity (taking a walk, riding bicycles, or preparing a meal for example)

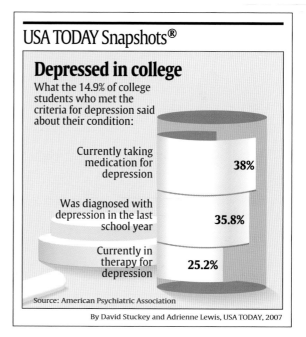

USA TODAY Snapshots®

Depressed in college

What the 14.9% of college students who met the criteria for depression said about their condition:

Currently taking medication for depression — 38%

Was diagnosed with depression in the last school year — 35.8%

Currently in therapy for depression — 25.2%

Source: American Psychiatric Association

By David Stuckey and Adrienne Lewis, USA TODAY, 2007

www.usatoday.com

USA TODAY
Life
SECTION D

September 27, 2010

From the Pages of USA TODAY

First weeks can be tough for college kids

A couple million sets of U.S. parents just realized a dream: They sent sons and daughters off to colleges. Most immediately set their sights on a new dream: attending graduation ceremonies at those colleges.

But right about now, some are getting the first clues that might not happen. A few know it won't—because their kids have already dropped out.

Going away to college is an exciting time. But for some students, the stress of accompanying changes becomes too much and leads to depression.

"I had a student leave the first week," says Marcus Hotaling, a psychologist who directs the counseling center at Union College in Schenectady, N.Y.

"It does happen," says Marjorie Savage, parent program director at the University of Minnesota-Twin Cities.

In fact, surveys by ACT (the non-profit company behind the ACT test) show one-third of freshmen do not become sophomores at the colleges where they started.

ACT doesn't track how many students drop out in less than a year, transfer to another school or return later. But just under half get degrees from the colleges where they first enrolled (within three years for associate degrees or five years for bachelor's degrees).

"The numbers are dreadful, and the freshman year is key," says James Boyle, president of College Parents of America in Arlington, Va.

That might strike panic into parents already getting distress signals:

- A drumbeat of negativity, via calls, e-mail, online status updates and other communications. A little homesickness is normal. But a student calling home "multiple times a day, crying or angry, overreacting to little things" is in trouble, Hotaling says. Savage says struggling freshmen say things like: "I can't sleep. I hate the food here. I don't like the people. It's not what I expected."
- No communication. "There's a lot of pressure to succeed," Hotaling says. So when things don't go well, students often don't want parents to know.
- Bad grades. Those are almost a rite of passage, "a reality check that typically comes in the first four weeks," Savage says. But if the bad news is still coming four weeks after that, she says, "you might start to worry more."

College students who live at home can show many of the same signs, Savage notes—and are at high risk for dropout because of the competing demands of school, home and, often, a job.

Also at high risk: students who came to school with a disability or a mental illness such as depression. Hotaling recalls one bright young man with a form of autism who came 3,000 miles [4,830 kilometers] and "didn't last the semester because he couldn't handle the social aspects." And sometimes leaving is the right thing, he says.

But, often, parents can help students stay put, without jumping in and taking over. "Stay in touch and provide coaching," Boyle says. Remind students that academic advisers, counselors and others are there to help, he says.

Encourage students to get involved in campus clubs, teams and activities, Savage says.

"Typically, if you give them a few weeks, they are going to adjust," Hotaling says. But, he adds, if you are concerned about safety—and, especially, suicide—don't hesitate to call the campus counseling center and ask for help.

—Kim Painter

Parents can help depressed teens by taking part in special one-on-one activities such as cooking or by giving their undivided attention and listening.

- Listen attentively without interrupting
- Give clear, simple instructions (such as when asking for chores to be done) so that there are no misunderstandings
- Give frequent praise and reward effort as well as achievement
- Encourage and guide the formation of friendships by planning an outing and inviting another teenager to go along
- Nurture a talent or a strength (look for a sports activity offered by the YMCA or a drawing class offered at an art studio, for example)

- Encourage trying a new activity at home that can be done without parental help (such as cooking dinner or planting and maintaining a vegetable garden)
- Give a loving hug

Teachers can also help by doing the following:

- Creating a classroom environment that fosters cooperation among students, with no tolerance for aggressive behavior or put-downs
- Planning classroom activities that allow all students to participate equally
- Avoiding classroom activities that encourage competition
- Giving frequent praise for students' efforts, while holding criticism to a minimum

CHAPTER SIX

THE POWER OF SELF-ESTEEM

Self-esteem relates to the way people feel about themselves. People with high self-esteem feel good about themselves. They take pride in their abilities and accomplishments, feel self-confident, think and make decisions independently of other people, and take on responsibilities and challenges. They tend to be well received by other people.

People who have low self-esteem do not feel good about themselves. They play down their abilities and accomplishments, lack self-confidence, feel powerless, become easily frustrated, and have difficulty thinking and making decisions on their own. They tend not to be well received by other people.

The way we feel about ourselves goes hand in hand with the control we have over our lives. When we believe in and value ourselves, we are more able to interact successfully with other people as well as to cope with life's disappointments. And the reverse is also true. Each time we meet with success in our relationships with others or in managing the ups and downs of our lives, we feel stronger and more self-confident. Our mood is brighter and our outlook on life becomes more positive.

DEPRESSION AND SELF-ESTEEM

Depression shrouds its victims in self-doubt, guilt, and despair. They begin to see only their weaknesses and failures, and these become huge and looming. Other people tend to avoid the depressed person and become critical of his or her negative and sometimes aggressive behavior. As the people around them pull away, depressed individuals become more and more convinced that they are worthless and bad.

From the Pages of USA TODAY

Study: Today's youth think quite highly of themselves

Today's teenagers and young adults are far more likely than their parents to believe they're great people, destined for maximum success as workers, spouses and parents, suggests a report comparing three decades of national surveys.

And these so-called Millennials or Gen Y young people may be heading for a fall when their self-esteem is punctured by reality, says psychologist Jean Twenge of San Diego State University [in California]. She examined changes from 1975 to 2006 in yearly surveys, given to thousands of high school seniors by University of Michigan researchers.

Compared with the Baby Boomers who were seniors in 1975, 12th graders surveyed in 2006 were much more confident they'd be "very good" employees, mates and parents, and they were more self-satisfied overall, say Twenge and co-author W. Keith Campbell of the University of Georgia. Between half and two-thirds of the Gen Y teens gave themselves top ratings, compared with less than half in their parents' generation. The report is in *Psychological Science*.

Boomer parents "are more likely than their parents were to praise children—and maybe overpraise them," Twenge says. This can foster great expectations or perhaps even smugness about one's chances of reaching "the stars" at work and in family life, she adds. "Their narcissism [self-absorption] could be a recipe for depression later when things don't work out as well as they expected."

But high self-esteem is more likely to protect them against depression, argues Brent Roberts, a psychologist at the University of Illinois at Urbana-Champaign. His studies of teenagers followed to age 21 found that low self-esteem in high school contributes to becoming more depressed later.

There's also evidence that having optimistic goals leads people to do better, Roberts says. "We don't know what these kids eventually are going to do. Maybe a lot of them will be great workers and better at family life than their parents were."

Still, kids and young adults with big egos could create problems for others, says Roy Baumeister, a psychologist at Florida State University who has studied self-esteem. "Many people who grew up in the '50s say, 'Nothing I did was ever good enough for my parents.' Now we're seeing the pendulum swing, and you hear from coaches and teachers who have been at it a while that kids have become more fragile. They don't take criticism well," he says.

"Thinking you're God's gift to the world is nice for you. It's a little harder for everyone else around you."

—Marilyn Elias

It is nearly impossible for them to feel important, in control, or hopeful. Their self-esteem falls to rock bottom.

SELF-HELP STRATEGIES TO BOOST SELF-ESTEEM AND MOOD

The treatments discussed in this book help to push aside the shroud of negative feelings associated with depression. As the negative feelings give way, people can take measures to begin to feel good about themselves and to establish an ongoing sense of well-being. Doing some of the things in the list that follows may help to distract someone from negative thoughts and help them to succeed and increase self-confidence. The end result will be a brighter outlook on life. Incorporating these strategies into everyday living may help to ward off the onset of future depressive episodes.

- Eat properly
- Exercise
- Get adequate rest
- Talk with family members
- Reduce stress
- Avoid procrastination
- Allow room for imperfections
- Keep a journal
- Replace negative thoughts with positive thoughts
- Make a list of strengths
- Enjoy a pet
- Plan outings
- Get involved in an enjoyable activity
- Join a club
- Get a job
- Organize belongings
- Do something nice for someone

- Do volunteer work

A properly balanced diet can provide the body with energy and foster a sense of well-being. Food contains the nutrients necessary for good physical and mental health. These nutrients are carried by the blood to all the organs of the body, including the brain. It is best not to skip meals or eat a lot of junk food.

Exercise can help to ease restlessness and can actually raise the levels of brain chemicals called endorphins, which elevate mood. Exercise also raises the heart rate and increases the amount of oxygen taken into the body, which contributes to good health. Being in shape also helps to nurture positive self-esteem.

Ideally, a good night's sleep is best. But when sleep is interrupted or insufficient, resting or napping during the day can help.

Setting aside time to talk with family members about events of the day or inner feelings can help keep the lines of communication open. Sound relationships are important in preventing future episodes of depression.

Research has shown that our attitude toward life can alter the amount of chemicals in the brain that affect the overall health of our bodies. If we feel anxious, for example,

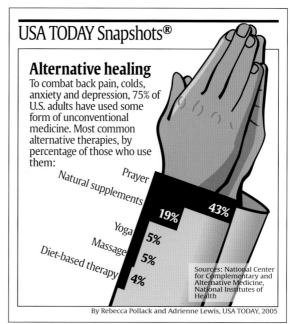

USA TODAY Snapshots®

Alternative healing
To combat back pain, colds, anxiety and depression, 75% of U.S. adults have used some form of unconventional medicine. Most common alternative therapies, by percentage of those who use them:

Prayer **43%**
Natural supplements **19%**
Yoga **5%**
Massage **5%**
Diet-based therapy **4%**

Sources: National Center for Complementary and Alternative Medicine, National Institutes of Health

By Rebecca Pollack and Adrienne Lewis, USA TODAY, 2005

our bodies produce extra stress hormones, which can work against sound health. The saying "Laughter is the best medicine" rings true. Laughing actually keeps the level of stress hormones down and can help in coping with difficult life events. Watching comedy shows on television or renting funny movies can lighten the mood. Listening to soothing music can also help to reduce stress.

Procrastination breeds stress. Worrying about assignments or chores that are left undone can burden the mind and create tension. Tackling tasks promptly can help to avoid anxiety.

Everyone makes mistakes and everyone has shortcomings. Trying to be perfect creates a lot of unnecessary worry. Accepting failure and being willing to try again can be much healthier. Setting reasonable goals can help. When the goal is attainable, success is more likely, and success bolsters self-esteem.

Worrying about problems can interfere with concentration and completion of tasks, including school assignments. Making a list of worries and writing down the feelings that accompany them

Many depressed people find that journaling helps them deal with feelings. Listing what is bothering them can help them let go. Listing what is going well can help them focus on the positive.

can often help to relieve the mind and make problems seem more manageable.

Erasing negative thoughts by replacing them with positive thoughts, such as good memories and plans for the future, can help break a pattern of negative thinking. Listing these positive thoughts on a piece of paper and then reading them when negative thoughts cloud the mind can improve a low mood.

A list of strengths can serve the same purpose. Strengths may include talents (such as being good in sports or playing a musical instrument well), achievements (such as winning a swimming race or learning how to bake a moist chocolate cake), special personality qualities (such as being especially patient with very young children or elderly people), interests that attract others (such as knowing a lot about astronomy or animals), and appealing physical features (such as shiny hair or white teeth). Focusing on strengths can help to lift falling self-esteem. Writing down fears and worries can make them seem more manageable and sometimes can even help you come up with solutions to a problem.

Focusing on personal strengths such as playing a musical instrument can help change a depressed person's way of thinking and improve self-esteem.

Playing with a pet can also be a mood elevator. The exercise you may get from it and time spent outside can help clear your mind. Playing with a pet, even someone else's, can help relieve stress and can often shift the focus away from life's problems.

Going out with family or friends and planning activities in advance can provide a welcome break from the daily worries of work and school. Outings to a concert, a movie, a museum, the beach, a lake, or an amusement park can be uplifting. Even taking a walk with a friend can help.

Taking a class or participating in a pleasurable activity such as dancing, gardening, cooking, sewing, sailing, skiing, developing a hobby, or drawing can bring joy. Many of these activities can be done with other people, which can help establish friendships.

Many schools offer after-school clubs, such as in drama, photography, gardening, or chess. A person can develop new interests and talents and form new friendships through participating in these clubs.

The benefits of taking on a part-time job include earning spending money, mastering a new skill, and working with other people. Not only can holding a job keep the mind positively focused, but it can also provide a sense of accomplishment.

Sometimes straightening a bedroom and organizing belongings can bring about a sense of well-being. Drawers and closets can be tidied, for example. Videos, compact discs, and books can be organized on a shelf. Putting together a photograph album of favorite photographs can also bring joy.

Doing a household chore without being asked or baking cookies for a family member or friend can help create positive inner feelings. Even paying someone a compliment can feel good. The added benefit of opening up to others is that others are likely to open up in return.

Spending a few hours each week or each month doing volunteer work can be extremely gratifying. Nursing homes, hospitals, libraries,

Many depressed people enjoy volunteering at a nursing home or with a local charity. Volunteering can help take your mind off your own problems and make you feel like part of a larger community.

and charitable organizations all welcome help from young people. In addition to feeling good about helping others, a skill may be learned that can be used in a paying job someday.

SUCCESS STORIES

Since receiving treatment for depression, all the young people profiled in this book have seen improvement in their lives. They are optimistic about the future.

KEVIN

Kevin was accepted to a prestigious college and is looking forward to entering the premedical program there. He is not yet ready to begin dating again. "I try not to dwell on what happened with Tracey," says Kevin. "When I start thinking about it, I push the thoughts away and try to focus on other things. It's not easy, but I'm trying. My volunteer work has helped keep my mind on other things. In my therapy sessions, we're working on building my self-confidence and I'm doing a little better. My parents have not been putting as much pressure on me either, which has helped." Kevin and his friend Joe have enrolled in a scuba diving class at the YMCA. They are planning to take a vacation together after they graduate high school.

LINDSAY

Lindsay is eating and sleeping normally again and no longer suffers from headaches. "I still miss my grandparents and always will," she says. "I miss all the fun times we had together and I miss having them at my special occasions, like my orchestra concerts and my birthday. But they sent me plane tickets to visit them over spring break, and I'm really looking forward to that. And they're planning to spend a couple of weeks with us over the summer. It's not the same as having them here in town every day, but at least it's something. I'm trying to accept things the way they are, and my therapy sessions are helping me." Lindsay has joined the junior garden club at her school. She is interested in learning more about plants and how to grow them. "I'd like to own a flower shop someday," she says. "I always feel happy when I'm around flowers and I love the beautiful arrangements that can be made with them."

"Lindsay is much more congenial now," says Lindsay's father. "She and her mother hardly ever argue anymore, which is a real pleasure. I used to be getting ready for work upstairs in the bedroom and hear them shouting at each other downstairs in the kitchen. I could feel my blood pressure rising. Now things are calm in the morning and it's such a relief."

SHARON

With the help of her therapist, Sharon is working on eating moderately and not purging. "It's a daily struggle," says Sharon. "This problem really has a hold on me. It's scary." In her therapy sessions, Sharon is working on building her self-esteem. Sharon's parents go to some of the therapy sessions and are learning to be more accepting of Sharon. They are learning to focus on her strengths, such as her abilities in music and art. Sharon has been attending book club discussions after school and has made a new friend. With her parents' help, she has planned some outings with this friend.

JORDYNN

Jordynn continues to enjoy acting and singing and got a part in the school play. She is getting along well with her stepfather, Peter, although she still feels sad that her father and mother are not together. "Dr. Goldy has helped me accept the new arrangement," says Jordynn. "My mom and Peter got me a puppy for Christmas, which made me really happy because I've wanted a dog for a long time. Whenever I feel down, I just turn to Rags. She does crazy things that make me laugh."

"I felt so guilty after I found out that Jordynn was depressed and that my marriage upset her so much," says Jordynn's mother. "I was torn because I love Jordynn, but I love Peter, too. I didn't want to hurt either one. How could I choose one over the other? I'm grateful to Dr. Goldy for helping us work things out. I try to plan things that Jordynn and I can do together, just the two of us, and Peter is good about giving us some private time. He understands Jordynn's needs. I think we're all going to be okay."

DOUG

The medication and therapy are helping Doug. He has cut off his relationship with his older friends and is working to get back on track.

"When my dad found out that I had all my problems, he decided to try to move back near us and now he has a job in the next town. It's only a ten-minute drive, so we get to see him a lot more. We get to spend every other weekend with him, and sometimes we see him during the week, too. We've done a lot of canoeing and hiking in the woods, which I really enjoy. It gives me something to look forward to. Like me, my mom has been diagnosed with depression and has been going to therapy. I think it's helping her. Even though we still argue sometimes, we're getting along better, and I'm getting along better with my brother, too."

ANTHONY

Anthony's bipolar disorder is controlled with lithium. His psychiatrist monitors the medication and helps Anthony with psychotherapy. His doctor recommended that he reduce the stress in his life. He suggested that Anthony live at home and go to school part-time at a nearby community college for now. "My doctor told me that exercise helps to reduce stress, so I've joined a volleyball league at my new school," says Anthony. "I've started to make friends on the team, and we sometimes go out for pizza after we play. Things are starting to come together for me, I think."

"After Anthony was diagnosed with manic depression, I realized that Anthony's father probably suffered from it, too," says Anthony's mother. "Anthony's father was killed in a motorcycle accident when Anthony was a baby. When I think back on the way he acted, there were signs of both mania and depression. There were times when he would ride his motorcycle for hours. He loved it. But he would sometimes ride so fast and recklessly. That's how he got in the accident—he lost control. And then there were other times when all he wanted to do was watch TV, and I don't even think he was really watching it. At those times, he wouldn't be interested in doing anything else, not even riding his

motorcycle. And he would sleep a lot, too. I'd have an awful time waking him up to go to work. We know from what Anthony's psychiatrist has told us and books I've read that manic depression can be inherited. I think Anthony inherited it from his father."

MOLLY

Molly's father is being treated with medication and psychotherapy, and his depression has begun to lift. He has been able to participate more in his children's lives. The responsibilities of the house, cooking, and younger children no longer fall on Molly's shoulders. The psychiatrist recommended that Molly's father hire outside help, and he found a woman to come in for a few hours every day to help with the chores. Molly's father does the grocery shopping and runs errands. "For the first time in a very long time, I'm able to just be a kid," says Molly. "I'm trying to enjoy being a teenager, and I'm starting to reestablish some friendships. I had wanted to go away to college, but I don't think I'm ready. I meet with my psychiatrist regularly and I think that's important. I've recently started dating someone from school and I really like him. He's a senior, too. We had our graduation pictures taken and mine came out pretty well. I think my mom would have liked them. I miss her."

GLOSSARY

anorexia nervosa: an eating disorder characterized by an intense fear of being overweight that causes the individual to eat very little food and experience dangerous weight loss

antidepressant medication: mood-regulating medication used to relieve depression

attention deficit/hyperactivity disorder: a condition that involves several related symptoms that fall into three main categories: inattention, impulsiveness, and hyperactivity

atypical depression: a form of depression characterized by oversleeping and overeating, decreased energy, and extreme sensitivity to rejection

axon: a thin projection on the end of a neuron that transmits messages to other neurons

behavioral therapy: a type of psychotherapy that treats depression as learned behavior that can be unlearned

bipolar disorder: alternating periods of feeling extremely happy and extremely depressed; also called manic depression or bipolar depression

bulimia nervosa: an eating disorder characterized by bingeing on food and then purging by vomiting or using laxatives

cognitive therapy: a type of psychotherapy based on the idea that people who think negatively about themselves, the world, and the future will develop feelings of despair. Patients are taught to replace negative thoughts with positive thoughts.

delusion: a false belief

dopamine: a neurotransmitter that helps to regulate mood

dysthymia: a mild form of depression that lasts two or more years

electroconvulsive therapy (ECT): a treatment for severe depression that involves passing a low-voltage electrical current through the brain; also called shock therapy

family therapy: a type of psychotherapy that involves the entire family participating in a therapy session to discuss problems and improve communication

hallucination: an imaginary vision

interpersonal therapy: a type of psychotherapy that is based on the idea that people become depressed because of problems that arise within relationships with family or friends

lithium: a medication given to people with bipolar disorder

major depression: a severe mood disorder that involves a group of symptoms that interfere with everyday functioning

manic depression: alternating moods characterized by extreme highs and lows; also called bipolar disorder

monoamine oxidase: an enzyme in the nervous system that breaks down neurotransmitters

neurons: nerve cells

neurotransmitters: brain chemicals that carry messages from one neuron to another

norepinephrine: a type of neurotransmitter that helps to regulate mood

obsessive-compulsive disorder: an anxiety disorder characterized by a persistent thought or impulse (obsession) to perform some activity repetitively, or compulsively

psychiatrist: a medical doctor who specializes in the treatment of mental, emotional, and behavioral disorders

psychologist: a person educated in the science of the mind and behavior who is trained in counseling people with mental, emotional, and/or behavioral disorders

psychotherapy: the treatment of emotional disorders that involves talking with a therapist to understand and resolve conflicts

receptors: molecules on the surface of neurons that receive messages from neurotransmitters

reuptake: reabsorption of a neurotransmitter by the neuron that released it

seasonal affective disorder: a form of depression that usually occurs during the fall and winter months when there is decreased sunlight

self-esteem: confidence in and satisfaction with one's self

serotonin: a type of neurotransmitter that helps to regulate mood

stress: tension that affects the body and the mind

synapse: a tiny, fluid-filled gap between neurons across which messages are carried by neurotransmitters

therapist: a professional who works with people to solve problems, discuss feelings, or change behavior. Psychiatrists, psychologists, and social workers are therapists.

therapy: a treatment designed to bring about healing

RESOURCES

American Academy of Child and Adolescent Psychiatry (AACAP)
3615 Wisconsin Ave. NW
Washington, DC 20016-3007
1 (800) 333-7636
http://www.aacap.org
AACAP is dedicated to educating families, teachers, and other concerned individuals about mental health issues facing children and adolescents to promote early identification and treatment and to encourage funding for scientifically based research.

Depression and Bipolar Support Alliance (DBSA)
730 N. Franklin St., Suite 501
Chicago, IL 60610-7224
1 (800) 826-3632
http://www.dbsalliance.org
DBSA's mission is to educate the public about depression and bipolar disorder. This organization stresses that depression and bipolar disorder are treatable, and it strives to help patients and their families find help. Founded in 1985, DBSA has seventeen state organizations and more than four hundred chapters across the United States.

Depression and Related Affective Disorders Association (DRADA)
Johns Hopkins Hospital
600 North Wolfe St.
Baltimore, MD 21287-7381
(410) 955-4647
http://www.drada.org
DRADA is a nonprofit organization whose mission is to alleviate the suffering associated with depression by assisting self-help groups, providing education and information, and lending support to research programs.

The International Foundation for Research and Education on Depression (iFred)
PO Box 17598
Baltimore, MD 21297-1598
(800) 442-HOPE (4673)
http://www.ifred.org
This nonprofit organization helps to further research into the causes of depression. It also supports those dealing with depression and works to educate the public and combat the stigma associated with depression. iFred has a hotline for people needing immediate help—(800) 442-HOPE will direct you to local resources.

National Alliance on Mental Health (NAMI)
3803 N. Fairfax Dr.
Suite 100
Arlington, VA 22203
(703) 524-7600
http://nami.org
NAMI is the largest grassroots organization in the United States dedicated to improving the lives of individuals and families affected by mental illness. Their activities focus on support, education, and advocacy. In addition to the national organization, there are more than one thousand state and local groups across the United States. NAMI's information helpline, (800) 950-NAMI, is monitored by trained volunteers who can provide information, referrals, and support to anyone who has questions about or is affected by serious mental illness.

National Mental Health Association (NMHA)
2001 N. Beauregard St., 12th Floor
Alexandria, VA 22311
(800) 969-6642
http://www.nmha.org
NMHA has more than three hundred affiliates nationwide. The organization strives to educate the public about mental health issues, promote research in this field, and provide community service for people with mental illnesses and their families.

National Suicide Prevention Lifeline
(800) 273-TALK (8255)
www.suicidepreventionlifeline.org
If you or someone you know is in a suicidal crisis or emotional distress, the trained counselors at this organization can help. Calling the number connects you to the lifeline network closest to your location. The service is free and confidential and is available twenty-four hours a day, seven days a week.

SELECTED BIBLIOGRAPHY

Albrecht, Ava T., and Charles Herrick. *100 Questions and Answers about Depression*. Sudbury, MA: Jones & Bartlett, 2011.

Lucas, Eileen. *More Than the Blues? Understanding and Dealing with Depression*. Berkeley Heights, NJ: Enslow Publishers, 2010.

Mayo Clinic. "Depression." MayoClinic.com. February 11, 2010. http://www .mayoclinic.com/health/depression/DS00175 (October 11, 2010).

O'Connor, Richard. *Undoing Depression: What Therapy Doesn't Teach You and Medication Can't Give You*. New York: Little, Brown, 2010.

WebMD. "Depression Health Center." WebMD.com. N.d. http://www.webmd.com/depression/default.htm (November 12, 2010).

FURTHER READING AND WEBSITES

Books

Denkmire, Heather. *The Truth about Anxiety and Depression*. New York: Facts on File, 2010.

Farrar, Amy. *ADHD*. Minneapolis: Twenty-First Century Books, 2011.

Hyman, Bruce M., and Cherry Pedrick. *Anxiety Disorders*. Minneapolis: Twenty-First Century Books, 2006.

Irwin, Cait. *Monochrome Days: A Firsthand Account of One Teenager's Experience with Depression*. New York: Oxford University Press, 2007.

Langwith, Jacqueline, ed. *Perspectives on Diseases and Disorders: Depression*. Farmington Hills, MI: Greenhaven Press, 2009.

LERNER

SOURCE

Expand learning beyond the printed book. Download free, complementary educational resources for this book from our website, www.lerneresource.com

Websites

American Psychological Association (APA)
http://www.apa.org

The APA is a scientific and professional organization that represents psychology in the United States. It is the largest association of psychologists worldwide. The organization works to share it's members' psychological knowledge to benefit society and improve people's lives. The website's *Emotional Health* page provides information on how emotional health leads to success in work, relationships, and health.

American Society for Adolescent Psychiatry (ASAP)
http://www.adolpsych.org

ASAP focuses on teen, adolescent, and young adult mental health issues. This professional network is dedicated to education development and advocacy of adolescents. Member psychiatrists can learn from one another as they help young people throughout North America. The website's *Teen Troubles* page (http://www. adolpsych.org/teen.html) provides articles geared to educate the public about teen-specific issues.

The Mayo Clinic
http://www.mayoclinic.com/health/teen-depression/DS01188

The Mayo Clinic, one of the best-known nonprofit medical institutions in the United States, has comprehensive information on depression, including information on symptoms, causes, risk factors, complications, tests and diagnosis, treatment, lifestyle remedies, alternative medicine, coping and support, and prevention.

National Alliance for Research on Schizophrenia and Depression (NARSAD)
http://www.narsad.org/

NARSAD raises money from donors around the world and invests it directly in research projects in mental health. The NARSAD website provides information on depression, anxiety, obsessive-compulsive disorder, and schizophrenia, including the latest research, feature articles, and information for people with depression and those who want to help them.

TeensHealth
http://kidshealth.org/teen

TeensHealth is a project of the Nemours Foundation, one of the largest nonprofit organizations devoted to children's health. The site provides information on a wide range of physical, emotional, and behavioral issues that affect children and teens. For information on depression, go to http://kidshealth.org/teen/your_mind/ mental_health/depression.html.

INDEX

ABOUT THE AUTHOR

Wendy Moragne is a former teacher who has written on medical topics. She is currently practicing law and lives in Moorestown, New Jersey.

PHOTO ACKNOWLEDGMENTS

The images in this book are used with the permission of: © Science VU/DOE/Visuals Unlimited, Inc., pp. 1, 3; © ColorBlind Images/Iconica/Getty Images, p. 5; © Radius Images/Alamy, p. 11; © Eight Arts Photography/Alamy, Inc., p. 15; © Image Source/ Getty Images, p. 17; © Todd Strand/Independent Picture Service, p. 21; © Laura Westlund/Independent Picture Service, p. 22; © Elyse Lewin/Photographer's Choice/Getty Images, p. 24; © Jupiterimages/Brand X Pictures/Getty Images, p. 26; © Dennis MacDonald/Alamy, p. 27; © Eileen Blass/USA TODAY, pp. 28, 48;© Bubbles Photolibrary/Alamy, p. 32; © Nancy Ney/Photodisc/Getty Images, p. 35; © Ron Levine/Riser/Getty Images, p. 37; © Comstock/Getty Images, pp. 39, 102; © Image Source/Getty Images, p. 41; © Cheryl Gerber/USA TODAY, p. 42; © Katye Martens/ USA TODAY, p. 46; © Stefan Wettainen/Johner Images/Getty Images, p. 50; © Tetra Images/Getty Images, p. 54; © Bruce Ayres/Stone/Getty Images, p. 64; © Manchan Manchan/White/Photolibrary, p. 66; © Elena Elisseeva/Dreamstime.com, pp. 68, 104 (left); © Judy G. Rolfe/USA TODAY, p. 71; © Will & Deni McIntyre/Photo Researchers, Inc., p. 75; © Cyberonics, Inc. via Getty Images, p. 76; © Medical Body Scans/Photo Researchers, Inc., p. 77; © Bradley C. Bower/Bloomberg via Getty Images, p. 78; © ACE STOCK LIMITED/Alamy, p. 87; © INSADCO Photography/ Alamy, p. 89; © iStockphoto.com/Stephen Finn, p. 91; © Bfphoto/Dreamstime.com, p. 98; © FotoKIA/Photolibrary/Getty Images, p. 104 (right); © Branko Kosteski/ Dreamstime.com, p. 110; © Junial/Dreamstime.com, p. 111; © David Grosman/ Alamy, p. 113.

Front cover: © Science VU/DOE/Visuals Unlimited, Inc.